Praise for Conscious Girlfriend

Your *Did You Order the U-Haul Yet?* vi_____ ____
nitely gave me a new angle from which to view conflict resolution
and closeness in my own relationships. The conscientiousness, inclu-
siveness and emotional honesty were so refreshing. – Sid March,
Managing Editor, Lesbian.com

Nan and I are going strong - 8 months into building our conscious
GF relationship. I LOVE the work you do. I feel like we are the proof
it works. – Cherie Taylor

I watched your video thinking I was doing research for The Lesbian
Conference and voila, what you were saying was for me, a lesbian
who is in a very good relationship but knows it can be better. I really
feel the authenticity and expertise of your words. – Sandra Sick,
Executive Director, The Lesbian Conference

It's only Week 4 of the Roadmap Course, and I can feel huge shifts…
I'm just blown away by this work and how it's put together, how
effective it is, how thoughtful it is. The course is easily worth three or
four times what I paid for it. – C.S.

I have to echo so many other women about how incredible the Roadmap Course is. There've been so many epiphanies. Thank you from
the bottom of my heart. I've done a lot of work yet there were so many
areas I was still really stuck in. Trying to read about relationships in
general, rather than lesbian relationships, I just haven't gotten these
insights before. –A.H.

I've been religiously doing the homework in the Roadmap Course,
and I'm noticing that the people coming into my life are much
healthier! … It's very neat that with all the homework, I can already
see a difference. I've been blessed enough to meet women that have
really added to my life… but I haven't had a good "picker." And now
I'm learning how to look for what I need, and also be more conscious
of the other person's needs. It's amazing. Thank you! – M.A.

I feel that you have constructed this course in such a great way – everything is so carefully thought out. I'm very appreciative of that. Now I feel like I'm equipped for something that I was never equipped for before. – G.H.

Your contribution to us as individuals and as a community is priceless. I am deeply grateful for the work you do, and the generosity of your spirit in all that you share. You are a gift to us all. Blessings always, Vera

I absolutely love what you two are doing for our community, and I cannot thank you both enough. Keep up the great work. – Magda Santiago

I am looking forward to growing with Conscious Girlfriend and will be a big advocate for the wonderful work that you do. This world is blessed to have loving people like you two, who share your love selflessly. – Rafaella

This is the best thing that's ever happened in the lesbian community. – Yolanda

I feel really thrilled because I've been floundering for a long time, and the two of you are naming the thing I want but I was feeling like I was crazy because I hadn't really seen it before... It feels incredibly validating to have found your work. It's really difficult to find visible queer relationships that I would emulate. I feel like now I can give light to the vision I had, instead of stuffing it and belittling it. I suddenly feel like I'm back on my own journey in a wonderful new world. Thank you, thank you, thank you! – A. N.

Your leadership in this sensitive area is such a boon for our community... I spent a lot of time last night looking through all the rich material on your website. It is a treasure trove. – Barbara

I feel so much stronger about dating after taking the Roadmap Course... I don't feel like I'm damaged goods. I have so much more to offer other women now. – Doris Hollings, L.Ac

CONSCIOUS
LESBIAN
DATING & LOVE

A ROADMAP TO FINDING THE RIGHT PARTNER
AND CREATING THE RELATIONSHIP OF YOUR DREAMS

RUTH L. SCHWARTZ, PH.D. &
MICHELLE MURRAIN, PH.D.

SIX DIRECTIONS PRESS

Six Directions Press,
Oakland, California

ISBN: 978-0-9965588-2-2

Cover design by Karen Davies (KarenDaviesDesign@gmail.com) and Ruth L. Schwartz. Book design by Lisa Despain (ebookconverting.com).

Manufactured in the United States of America.

Library of Congress Cataloging-in-Publication Data
Schwartz, Ruth L.
Murrain, Michelle
Conscious Lesbian Dating & Love: A 12-Week Roadmap for Finding the Right Partner, *Being* the Right Partner, and Creating the Relationship of Your Dreams
By Ruth L. Schwartz, Ph.D. & Michelle Murrain, Ph.D.

Acknowledgments

We are deeply grateful for the many people and forces who have aided us in writing this book – and who helped us do the learning, growing and healing that led to Conscious Girlfriend.

Both of us thank:

Gay and Katie Hendricks – Thank you for the visionary words and perspectives in your books *Conscious Loving, The 10-Second Miracle, Attracting Genuine Love, Learning to Love Yourself,* and many others. And thank you for your amazing coaching training, and for your pioneering somatic work and guidance, including development of the Fear Melters. You have changed our lives.

All of our students and clients – Thank you for sharing your lives, hearts and challenges with us so fully, teaching us so much, and allowing us the privilege of witnessing you as you open yourself more fully to the conscious love you want. We couldn't do this work without you – and we wouldn't want to.

Ruth thanks:

Isa Gucciardi – Thank you for bringing profound healing into my life, and opening the doors for me to access so much more.

All my ex-lovers (you know who you are.) – Thank you so much for all you taught me about love, loss, passion and the damning effects of processing. I apologize for not having better skills with which to love you.

Michelle, my dearly beloved partner in life and work – Every day you continue to show me more of what is possible, and you have enriched my time on this planet beyond measure. I treasure your wise, gentle spirit, your tender heart, your brilliant mind, and your deep commitment to consciousness and healing. (And I also really appreciate the fact that you get my silly sense of humor.)

Michelle thanks:

Arinna Weisman, friend and teacher, for introducing me to Buddhist practice, and showing me how it could make my life so much wider, deeper, and happier.

Eric Kolvig, for suggesting that I practice Metta meditation every day for a year.

Joellyn Monahan, who helped me understand my calling.

K., the-almost (you know who you are) for helping me learn the consequences of not being able to express my feelings and desire. I so wish I had done better by you.

And my love, Ruth, who loves me so deeply and well. You have taught me so much about the possibilities of love. I so appreciate the relentlessness of your growing spirit, your sharp mind, your courage and commitment, and your silliness.

Notes from the Authors

The stories in this book are true. However, we have changed the names and some identifying details of our ex-partners, clients and students, in order to protect their privacy.

Ruth was the primary writer of this book, so a disproportionate share of the stories herein are hers. Where there is an "I" in this book, it belongs to Ruth.

Since founding Conscious Girlfriend in early 2014, we're thrilled to have been able to help thousands of lesbians and queer women learn to date more consciously and wisely, and create the healthy, fulfilling relationships they've always wanted. We look forward to helping many more through this book, as well as through our coaching, articles, videos, teleclasses, online classes, retreats and more.

We'd love to support you in *your* journey to the relationship you most want. We offer free resources at consciousgirlfriend.com – and when you sign up for our mailing list, you'll get access to all our latest offerings!

Table of Contents

INTRODUCTION

Why A Conscious Approach?

"*Are you interested in a conscious approach to lesbian dating and relationships?*"

I asked that question over and over to the thousands of lesbians and queer women streaming by the Conscious Girlfriend booth at a recent women's music festival.

A few said, "No!" and quickly walked on.

A few said, "Yes, absolutely. I try to do that already."

But the majority said, "I don't know. What exactly does that mean?"

This book is for all lesbians and queer women: those who say "Yes," those who say "I don't know," and even those who are tempted to just walk away.

If you're already committed to conscious relationships, this book will help you apply the learning you've done elsewhere, as well as give you some powerful new lesbian-centric tools. Our framework is compatible with Buddhist practice, Non-Violent Communication, Landmark, 12-step work, therapy, and most other forms of healing and consciousness work, and it will help you integrate that work more fully in your dating and relationship life.

For many of us, intimate relationships are the final frontier. A lot of women have great lives in other ways, yet still struggle with old patterns in the dating and relationship arena. This was true for Michelle and me for a long time, too. So if that's the case for you, our most important message to you is: *it can change!*

If you're not sure what a conscious approach to lesbian dating and love means, this book will introduce you to a step-by-step path to dating wisely and creating the kind of relationship you truly want. Along the way, you'll learn many skills and ways of being that will enhance all your other relationships, too, including your relationship with yourself.

Becoming what we call a "conscious girlfriend" will take some learning and effort on your part. It's not magic, and it's not instant. *But it also doesn't have to be all that hard.*

In fact, if you add up the number of weeks, months or years you've already spent either unhappily single, getting over a breakup, or struggling with a painful relationship, you'll probably see that the Conscious Girlfriend approach is actually far *easier* than what you've already been doing – and also brings you far more happiness in return for your effort.

Although dismantling old patterns and learning new skills can feel intimidating at first, you are definitely capable of it. We have tools to walk you through the process. And the rewards are well worth it!

Now, if you're in the third category – someone whose immediate response to the question, "Are you interested in a conscious approach to lesbian dating and relationships?" would be to say "No," and keep walking – I'm especially glad you're reading this.

Since Michelle and I started Conscious Girlfriend, we've spoken with many lesbians and queer women who have been so hurt and disillusioned by relationships that they've given up on love. They've concluded that lasting, happy relationships must just be a myth – or at the very least, must be possible only for other, luckier women.

When you've repeatedly tried to do something and it hasn't worked, it does make sense to stop. As Albert Einstein said, the definition is insanity is doing the same thing over and over, and expecting different results.

But rather than giving up on love altogether, another sane alternative is to get some education and training, so that you can acquire whatever skills you're missing.

After all, you'd probably do that in any other area of your life. For instance, if you wanted to build a house, or learn to bake bread, or get good at doing the Argentine tango, you might take a class, watch some videos, find a mentor or teacher, or at least read a book.

Many things worth doing are hard to figure out on your own, yet completely learnable when you get the right guidance and support.

The truth is, if you don't have the right skills, the house you build won't be a good shelter, the bread you bake won't rise, and your dance steps will be clumsy. Similarly, without the right skills, your relationships might feel good at first, but they're likely to fall apart or cause pain within a few months or years.

But once you *do* have the right skills, relationships get much easier. *In fact, having a happy, healthy, lasting relationship doesn't have to be hard.*

There are two reasons why most relationships *are* hard (and aren't ultimately happy, healthy or lasting): 1) You're not with the right person, and/or 2) You're not yet the right person yourself. In other words, you don't know how to fully hold onto yourself within a relationship, communicate and navigate differences in healthy ways, and build trust and intimacy.

But both of these problems are solvable. You can learn how to find and choose the right partner, and you can learn how to *be* the right partner, too.

Becoming A Conscious Girlfriend

In order to find and choose the right partner, and to *be* the right partner yourself, you need to become what we call a "conscious girlfriend." This means becoming more conscious of all the many choices you make both in the dating process, and when you're actually in an intimate relationship.

When you're not conscious of what you're doing and why you're doing it, you end up operating on default or automatic pilot. This leads to doing things in ways that really don't fit who you are or what you want, sometimes without even realizing it. You may be living out the script of your parents' relationship, repeating your own patterns over and over, or doing what your partners want (or what you think they want – even while they're trying to do what they think *you* want!)

You might be choosing women whom you have to take care of – and then feeling frustrated that you're always taking care of them. (I used to do that.)

You might be trying to take care of your partners, or giving yourself up, in ways that don't even feel good to the other person. (I used to do that, too!)

You might be stuffing your feelings – or blowing up at your partner – because you don't know how to communicate your emotions and needs in healthy ways. Or you might be spending hours in exhausting, draining "processing" that never seems to get you anywhere. (One of my ex-partners dubbed me "the processing queen...")

You might be blaming her for whatever doesn't feel good between you, or blaming yourself, or both, rather than taking responsibility for your needs and working constructively to get them met.

Most of the couples we coach have been doing one or more of these things – so both partners end up feeling hurt, frustrated, angry and exhausted, and neither one is getting what she wants.

In contrast, once you bring full awareness to the process of dating and love, you can learn to make the choices that truly serve your happiness and well-being.

What do we mean when we say "the right partner?" What factors make someone the right partner for you – or the wrong one?

And what's really involved in healthy communication? What does it take to build trust, connection and intimacy, not just in the "honeymoon phase," but over the course of years and even decades – so that rather than getting stale, love can keep on growing stronger?

How is it possible for two different people, with different needs and preferences, to *both* get what they want?

Why do so many women try so hard to make love work, yet end up hurting each other? And what's the alternative?

We'll be talking much more about all of this in the chapters to come. But what we can tell you right now is that lasting, happy, healthy lesbian love is not a myth or an impossible dream. It's realistic and achievable. It just takes learning how.

Which Puzzle Pieces Are You Missing?

If you've struggled in relationships, the whole process of dating and love may seem like a confusing mystery. It might even feel like it's out of your hands, as if everything rests on who you happen to meet, or on some other factor you can't predict or control.

That feeling is understandable, *but it's not true.* We've seen over and over again that if your relationships go wrong – or if you've been single for long periods of time, despite wanting a relationship –

it's usually because you're missing some key pieces of the dating or relationship puzzle.

Check out the list below to see which pieces you're missing.

- It may be that you're not completely over a previous partner, or healed from a breakup. *This gets in the way of your being truly emotionally available, and finding an emotionally available partner, too.*

- It may be that you don't understand the anatomy of relationships – especially lesbian relationships – and why the early "honeymoon stage" can be so misleading. *This leads to making commitments to the wrong women.*

- It may be that you haven't known how to recognize red flags and steer away from them. *This leads to choosing women who either aren't right for you, or who are just bad news in general.*

- It may be that you've got some old beliefs about relationships that are getting in your way. *This can lead to your staying away from relationships entirely, or creating a relationship different from what you want.*

- It may be that you've never clearly defined your relationship vision and priorities. *When you don't know exactly what you want, it's almost impossible to find it.*

- It may be that you haven't known how to work out common conflicts, like when one person wants more closeness, and the other needs more space. *This leads to a lot of confusion, struggle and pain.*

- It may be that you don't have all the skills you need to build lasting connection in a relationship. *Lack of skills will destroy a relationship, even if the partners are otherwise well-matched. .*

- It may be that you're wary because lesbian breakups are so painful, and you're not sure you can take another one. *This fear can keep you from entering a relationship at all – or, ironically, can lead you to choose the wrong women repeatedly as a kind of self-fulfilling prophesy.*

The good news is, once you get clear on the puzzle pieces you need, you can clear up whatever's been blocking you, gain the skills you need, and become truly ready for the love you want. And we've seen over and over again that once someone is truly ready, that love shows up!

The Only Barrier Is You

Many of our clients and students worry that there's something about them that keeps them from being able to find the love they want.

We often hear women say things like this:

- *I'm too old. All the good ones in my age group are taken.*
- *I'm too young. Most women in my peer group don't have these skills, and older women don't take me seriously.*
- *I have children. Most women don't want to be with someone with kids.*
- *I have too many health problems.*
- *My income is too low.*
- *I'm not in good enough shape.*
- *I'm disabled / deaf / sight-impaired / have a pacemaker / have a cancer history / use a CPAP machine / have false teeth.*
- *There aren't enough lesbians in my town/city/state/province/ country.*
- *I'm bisexual.*

- *I'm a transwoman.*

- *I came out later in life.*

- *I'm not physically attractive.*

- *My childhood was too unhappy.*

These kinds of fears can run very deep. We understand.

But the truth is that whatever your specific circumstances may be, they do not have the power to keep you from love.

Sure, there are some women out there who might not be interested in you because of one of the factors listed above. But there are also many for whom it wouldn't be a barrier.

For instance, we hear from huge numbers of women over 60, and many over 70, who are looking for a loving relationship in which to spend the rest of their lives.

We also hear from many younger women who recognize that only a deeper approach to dating and relationships will bring them what they want.

All of us have health problems as we age, if not before. Health issues don't have to keep us from loving and being loved.

Women of all income brackets are looking for deep relationships – and while some want a partner with a similar level of financial resources, for others it's not a concern.

We could go on and on. The point is, whatever your particulars might be, you're not single because no one would want you (or because no one "good" would want you.) You're single because you're not ready for the kind of love you want.

How do we know? Because when you *are* ready, it will happen.

Once you learn and fully use the skills we'll cover in this book, you'll be able to find a truly compatible partner and build that connection into a strong, lasting relationship.

We Speak From Experience

We've been together since 2006, and we have an amazing friendship, partnership and marriage. Our own relationship is our best example and living proof of our approach. We practice what we preach. We walk our talk. We make use of all the skills we teach. That's how we know they work, and that's why our relationship thrives.

In early 2014 we created Conscious Girlfriend, an organization dedicated to helping lesbians and queer women learn how to date wisely and love well. Since then, we've been thrilled to get to help thousands of women gain the skills to have the lasting, loving relationships they want.

Our work makes use of both our professional backgrounds, and our own decades of personal experience in the lesbian/queer community. Michelle has a Ph.D. in Neuroscience; she has also had a Buddhist practice for over 25 years, and attended seminary. I have a Ph.D. in Transpersonal Psychology, and have trained extensively studied hypnotherapy, shamanism and other forms of transformational healing. We like to say that our approach to dating and relationships combines science, psychology and spirit.

But our professional training alone could never have gotten us here. We learned much of we know the hard way – and that's why we're so committed to making it easier for other members of our community.

Here's what our relationship looks like now: we trust each other, adore each other, respect and support each other, and also empower each other to keep growing, keep becoming more and more of our full selves.

We spend a lot of intimate time together – and a lot of time working together on Conscious Girlfriend – and also time apart to nurture our different interests, friendships, and need for alone-time.

As our needs change, we recognize what we're feeling, speak openly to each other, listen deeply, and find ways to let our relationship change, too. That's what keeps our love feeling alive to both of us, and lets us stay fully alive within it.

Our relationship doesn't feel like hard work. In fact, it actually feels easy most of the time. It supports our creativity and our work in the world, while also giving us companionship and nourishment.

But this kind of love did not come automatically to either one of us. And we certainly didn't see this kind of love around us when we were kids!

Ruth's Story

I grew up in a household filled with fighting and tension. My dad was a brilliant, charming man who also had affairs and went into rages. He often yelled, sometimes threw things, and occasionally shook or hit my mother. My mom was a timid 18-year-old when I was born, still struggling with being away from her own mother. So, from an early age, I did my best to parent her and my younger sister.

My father left when I was 12, and my mom's second marriage was also to an abusive man. After they got engaged, I graduated from high school early and left home at 16 so I wouldn't have to live with him. As a lonely teenager I began my own pattern of drama-filled relationships. I fell in love many times, but despite all my effort, the relationships never seemed to work over the long haul.

I see now that I had no idea how to choose a partner wisely. Mostly, I just followed wherever my attractions led. If there was chemistry – and then if the other woman showed me some vulnerability, which made me want to take care of her and heal her – I thought that would be enough to make love last. It wasn't.

In my first relationship, I felt stifled, and didn't understand why. I ended up having affairs, just as I had seen my father do.

Later I broke that pattern, but I made other choices that led to unhappiness. I gave too much too much. I chose women who were deeply wounded, and tried to heal them. I started fights because I didn't know how to cope with the sadness and anger that sometimes washed through me. I often blamed my partners when I got triggered or felt unhappy, rather than seeing my own part in things.

Mostly, I was the one to leave. But in my late thirties, I fell madly in love with someone I hoped to be with forever – and was completely devastated when she ended our relationship, ten months in. Then I had two more brief relationships, each of which ended in heartbreak after about a year.

Those relationships brought me to my knees. Finally, in my early forties, I committed myself to learning whatever I needed to learn to be able to love differently. I read a lot of books, did a lot of healing work, and essentially put myself through my own self-created Conscious Girlfriend program over a period of several years.

I was 44 when I met Michelle and started the first truly fulfilling, healthy relationship of my life. Since I had my first relationship at the tender age of thirteen, that means it took me more than 30 years to learn how to have the kind of love I'd always wanted. I still count myself lucky – but I wish something like Conscious Girlfriend had been available to me to help me get here more quickly and easily!

Michelle's Story

Michelle had her own difficult relationship patterns to break. A sensitive child with interests and values very different from those of her parents, she grew up feeling defective, and learned early on to escape into books and live in her head. She rarely knew what she was feeling, much less that she could actually communicate those feelings to someone else. When she got scared, she would withdraw and shut down.

As a teenager, Michelle felt so lost that she became a fundamentalist Christian in order to have a place to belong – but within a few years, she realized that church's dogmatism didn't fit her.

After coming out, Michelle had a crush on a friend for months, but never had the courage to say anything. Later, after that friend was already involved with someone else, she found out the feelings had been mutual. For a long time, she wondered what might have been… if only…

Then she began dating a woman with whom there were actual possibilities – but as soon as she started to have strong feelings, she got scared and ended the relationship.

Her first long-term relationship was with an abusive woman. Michelle financially supported her partner for more than five years, and also did all the shopping and cooking – yet despite that, her partner constantly criticized her. For most of that time, Michelle blamed herself and kept trying harder. She didn't leave until her partner became physically abusive.

Unfortunately, her next relationship wasn't much better. Although at least she didn't financially support that partner, she turned herself inside out trying to be the person she thought her partner wanted – but within a few years, her partner broke up with her without explanation.

At 43, Michelle finally realized that she would never have a good relationship until she learned how to love herself and know that she deserved love. So she, too, developed her own version of Conscious Girlfriend, devoting herself to practices that helped her literally re-wire her neural pathways, and went from being highly self-critical to having a healthy amount of self-love and self-compassion.

When she was 46, she posted the personals ad through which we met – and since then she's lived happily ever after. Well, not quite! You'll hear more about that later in this book.

We Didn't Just "Get Lucky"

In case you're thinking this ending sounds too much like Hollywood, we want to be very clear that we didn't just "get lucky." And although our relationship doesn't feel like hard work, it *does* require us to stay conscious. If we didn't, the same patterns that destroyed our earlier relationships would destroy this one, too.

If we didn't stay conscious:

I would blame Michelle for my feelings, rather than taking responsibility for them.

She would blame herself for my feelings, too. Then she'd feel overwhelmed and scared, withdraw and shut down.

Then I would get frustrated and triggered, and respond in ways that made her shut down even more.

Then she would feel stuck, broken and defective.

I would eventually leave her, bemoaning my ability to find someone who really "met" me, even while I failed to see my own part in what had happened.

Then she would feel like a failure and would think she was unlovable.

And then we would go find other women with whom to replicate these same patterns – or else give up on love entirely.

Ugh! It's not a pretty picture, is it?!

We know this is what would happen if we went unconscious, because even now we can sometimes feel the ghosts of those patterns rise up between us. Fortunately, we have the skills to recognize them when they come up, treat ourselves and each other with compassion, and dismantle them.

That's the difference being conscious can make.

In this book, we'll share a lot with you about the good, bad and ugly of our previous relationships. We'll tell you what we used to do wrong, and where it got us. And of course, we'll also tell you what we now do differently – the tools and choices that let us create and maintain the amazing relationship we now share.

The self-exploration and skill-building we'll guide you through in this book takes commitment and courage, but the rewards it yields are vast. *And if you commit to doing this process, it will work.* The only requirement is a willingness to learn. We'll teach you the rest.

CHAPTER 1

Conscious Lesbian Love: The Time is Now!

Lesbians and queer women have more social acceptance than ever before. We've finally won the right to marry throughout the United States, as well as many other countries. As a community, we're thrilled. We always knew our love was valid and healthy, and now much of the world has acknowledged that, too.

So now it's time to create the very best love we can.

Even if you've never had that kind of relationship before – or had it for a short time, and then went through the heartbreak of having it end.

Even if your past relationships have left you hurt, scared or doubtful about the possibility of long-term love.

Even if you're always attracted to the wrong women – or are afraid the right woman for you may not be out there at all.

Even if you're afraid you can't create the kind of love you want – or have wondered whether that kind of love is really possible for anyone.

Michelle and I *know* that happy, healthy, lasting lesbian love is possible for you. We know it because we've taught and coached many other lesbians and queer women how to find and create it – and most importantly, because we live it ourselves, every day.

And we know that becoming what we call a "conscious girl-friend" is the path that will get you there.

Your Past Relationship Problems Are Not Your Fault

If you've struggled to create the kind of love you've always wanted, you're not alone. Although some lesbians have managed to create deeply satisfying, joyful long-term bonds, they are in the minority. There's a tremendous amount of pain, confusion and fear about relationships in our community.

Why is it so hard?

Our work with thousands of women, as well as our study of neuroscience, psychology, and the recent history of the lesbian community, have shown us that lesbians do face some very specific challenges – as well as some unique opportunities – in the process of creating fulfilling long-term relationships.

One factor, of course, is the amount of homophobia and discrimination we've dealt with as a community and as individuals. Some of us have been rejected by our family members, our religions or our cultures. Some have lived in fear or hiding, been fired from jobs, been ostracized, gay-bashed, institutionalized, or subjected to "deprogramming."

Some of us have also internalized this prejudice and been scarred by self-hatred, shame about our sexuality, or the belief that there's something wrong with us for who and how we love.

These kinds of wounds don't disappear overnight. But with same-sex marriage finally legal, and more social acceptance in general, there is finally more room for us to begin to heal them.

Increased social acceptance will make our relationships easier – and sef-acceptance and pride in our lesbian selves is certainly another part of what makes us able to create the relationships we really want.

But lesbian relationships haven't just been difficult because of homophobia and oppression. They've also been hard for a number of other reasons.

The truth is, few people of *any* gender or orientation actually have the skills to choose a partner wisely, or create healthy, lasting love. It isn't just lesbians who need to learn how to love wisely – it's everyone!

The good news is, those skills are entirely learnable – and those of us who learn them pave the way for everyone else to have happier, more harmonious relationships too.

Another factor is that, as one of our students quipped, "Lesbian relationships are women, squared." Every lesbian relationship has two women in it, which means it has twice as much of the strengths *and* the challenges that women bring to love.

Studies show that women want and expect more from our relationships than men do. (That's why, in heterosexual relationships, the vast majority of visits to counselors – and also the vast majority of divorces – are initiated by women.) So when two women get together, both of us are likely to have high hopes and expectations – and when things don't go well, the pain can be crushing.

Does this mean our hopes and expectations are too high? No!

Instead, it means that we need to *do justice to those hopes and expectations* by learning how to choose our partners wisely, and bringing all the skills we need to our relationships.

It's Not About Fault. It's About Opportunity.

Every day we talk to lesbians who have had – or are presently in – painful, unsatisfying relationships.

Yet when we have the opportunity to talk to the partners or ex-partners of those same women, we often hear the same kind of pain, confusion and frustration from them, too.

In most cases, neither woman wanted or intended to hurt her partner. Usually both women are doing the best they can. They just don't have the right tools.

Whose fault is it? When something hurts, many of us tend to blame the other person. Some of us tend to blame ourselves. And some wisely try to rise above the tendency to blame altogether – and instead move into the freeing posture of self-responsibility.

Taking responsibility doesn't mean you take on blame. It means you acknowledge yourself as the co-creator of whatever's going on.

The truth is, it always "takes two to tango." In some way, you have contributed to any relationship dynamic you've ever been part of. This doesn't mean it was your fault, or that you wanted or deserved pain.

It *does* mean that you're more powerful than you may have realized. And when you take responsibility for whatever you've already created, *you can learn to create something different.*

Michelle: *I didn't want or deserve the criticism and abuse I got from my first partner. But I did co-create it by putting up with it, and staying with her for years even once it was clear to me that she was abusive. And that pattern only changed once I decided to change my own sense of self-worth – and then found the tools that helped me do that.*

Lesbians and queer women are the most amazing people we know. As a community, we're smart, passionate, bold, loving, resourceful, and infinitely courageous.

Every single one of us already demonstrated that courage by declaring ourselves lesbian, bisexual or queer – and that bravery was fueled by our deep desire to love and be loved by another woman.

Yet in spite of our courage and determination, our relationships often haven't worked out well. If that's true for you, it's not because there's anything wrong with you, and it's certainly not because there's anything wrong with being a lesbian. We believe lesbian relationships can be the very best intimate relationships in the world – but only when both women involved have the skills they need.

Most of us didn't get any useful instruction in relationships, period. You probably spent many years in school learning all kinds of things you never use, yet never took a single course in how to date wisely, state your needs clearly, listen well, resolve conflicts, or build intimacy.

Think about it. Someone undoubtedly taught you to drive. No one said to you, "When you meet the right car, you'll just automatically know what to do."

Yet with love, one of the most important aspects of our lives, most of us have gotten no help at all. No wonder the relationship "roads" are so scary out there!

Conscious Girlfriend is on a mission to change that. The skills you need are learnable. Bring us your motivation and willingness, and we'll walk you through the process.

You're Not Being Unrealistic. You Just Need Skills.

Women sometimes ask us, "Am I being unrealistic? Am I asking for too much? Is a happy, healthy, conscious relationship even possible? Can love actually stay strong?"

And our answers are: *No,* you're not being unrealistic. And *Yes,* the kind of deeply fulfilling, emotionally intimate long-term love you want *is* possible.

But creating a lasting relationship of that caliber won't happen by magic or by accident, and it *will* require some things from you.

Finding a great relationship – and keeping it great – doesn't depend on luck, magic or destiny. You don't have to just wait, wish or hope. You can *bring it about.* The power is in your hands.

Each dating and relationship choice you make is like a fork in the road. And each fork you take – each choice you make – will either bring you closer to happiness, or closer to heartbreak.

The good news is, you don't have to be perfect in order to learn how to make the right choices. You just have to be ready.

We know that deep, lasting true love is possible for you – even if you've never known how to find or create it before. We got here, and you can, too.

In this book, we'll walk you through our comprehensive 12-week program, The 12-Week Roadmap to Conscious Lesbian Dating & Lasting Love – to help you:

1) Understand the dating mistakes you may have made in the past, why they led to relationships that didn't work, and how to avoid those mistakes in the future.

2) Gain more clarity about what really happened in your past relationships, and why. We'll guide you through the process of understanding the part you played and forgiving yourself, so you'll be able to open your heart again and create a different future.

3) Identify what you most want and need from a relationship – what your unique vision is, and what constitutes real compatibility for *you.* You'll also learn which qualities all women who want happy, healthy long-term relationships need to have. (This is absolutely crucial, but it's not on the radar for most of us.)

4) Learn how to tell within the first few dates whether someone shares your vision and has the skills to carry it out or

not. You'll also find out how to gracefully stop dating her if she doesn't, or how to consciously continue exploring the connection if she does.

5) Develop the ability to speak, listen, resolve conflict and build intimacy in healthy ways, so you can keep love strong over the long haul.

There's a lot in this roadmap. But as we've said a few times already, the basic truth is that there are only two things you need to do in order to create lasting love: learn how to find the right partner, and how to *be* the right partner.

In other words, you need to be able to identify a woman who truly has the right stuff to co-create the kind of relationship you most want – and steer clear of all the women who might be cute, hot, smart, funny, interesting, spiritual and/or have other fine qualities, *but not ultimately be right for you.*

And in the process of finding the woman who *is* right for you – and as you actually build a relationship with her – you, too, need to be able to show up in ways that foster love, connection and intimacy. This book will teach you how.

In addition to the online 12-Week Roadmap to Conscious Lesbian Dating & Lasting Love, we offer online classes, coaching, videos, teleclasses, and live workshops and retreats. And we've had many success stories! We've helped women who had been single for years, or had a pattern of getting into unhealthy relationships, turn their love lives around completely, find a truly compatible partner, and begin the process of creating a beautiful life together.

And we've also helped couples on the brink of breakup – couples stuck in cycles of bickering, fighting or painful disconnection – turn their relationships around and find happiness with one another again.

We'd like to share a few stories with you, to give you a better idea of the transformation that has happened for our clients – and what can happen for you, too.

Meet a Few of Our Clients

Jill, 58, came to us after having chosen to be single for years following the painful breakup of her 18-year marriage. In less than three months of coaching, she forgave herself for her past mistakes, set boundaries with an unavailable woman who'd been leading her on, and got really clear what she wanted in a partner. Shortly after that, she met Cherie, and then brought Cherie to two coaching sessions so they could work through a few early glitches in their communication. Now, nearly a year later, they're going strong. Cherie recently emailed us, "I feel like we're the proof that Conscious Girlfriend works."

Sandy, 45, had been through a major heartbreak eighteen months before she started working with us. She told us she was drawn to women "with an edge" (it turned out that she meant women who were mean and controlling.) In less than 3 months of coaching, she broke off dating two women who fit her old pattern, developed much more self-love, and found a new partner with whom she shares a deep, joyful, drama-free love. Recently she let us know that they've moved in together, and she's amazed at how easily they navigate the kinds of differences that used to spell doom for her relationships. She says, "I want the two of you to dance at our wedding!"

Dorothy, 66, came to us after many years of what she called "lesbian train wrecks." We helped her pick through the rubble, identify the major dating mistakes she'd been making, and learn how to "fix her picker." She realized she'd had a pattern of choosing unstable, wounded women and then trying to heal them, rather than allowing herself to look for a healthy, equal partner. Now she knows the danger signs to watch out for, and has begun to date with a whole new level of clarity and confidence. "I know for sure I won't settle again," she says. "Because if I do, you'll kick my butt. Compassionately, of course, and at my request."

Melanie, 32, had a pattern similar to Dorothy's. She, too, had picked relationships in which she ended up having to be "the strong one." It was a pattern she knew well from her childhood – and one she was highly motivated to break, because she wanted children, and didn't want "a girlfriend who'll feel like just another child." With our help she moved through the internal blocks that had kept her stuck, met a compatible partner online, and is preparing to start her family within a truly healthy partnership.

Surya, 48, a longtime Buddhist practitioner, was frustrated because she'd found she couldn't translate her meditation skills into her daily lived relationship experience. Since Michelle has practiced Buddhism for over 25 years, she spoke Surya's language and helped her fully integrate her training in self-awareness and compassion. As a result, Surya reports that all her relationships are much smoother, and she and her ex-partner feel real hope about trying again. (And if they do, they plan to come to us for coaching.)

Nora, 59, practices non-violent communication, but found her communication skills seemed to desert her when she was interested in someone. It turned out that some of the missing pieces for her were self-compassion and the skill to work with her emotional triggers. Now she reports, "I feel more aligned inside and out, and I've started dating someone I feel really good about."

Felicity, 28, was excited to find us because she'd seen so few queer relationships that looked like ones she'd want to have. Her problem was a gap between the kind of communication she knew was possible, and the kind she felt able to have. With our help, she has narrowed that gap and says, "I finally feel like I can be myself around cute women in my age group! I'm also much clearer about who's a dating 'no' for me, and why."

Edwina, 60, is a therapist who was great at helping other couples solve their relationship problems, yet found herself unable to leave a relationship that didn't work for her. Every time she tried to separate from her partner, guilt or loneliness pulled her back. She didn't want to spend the rest of her life alone, but also knew she didn't want to "settle." With our help she finally made the break, and got clear on what she wanted for the future. Now, for the first time in her life, she feels ready to date while staying connected to herself and her own needs and vision.

Leila, 69, was battle-scarred from years of trying to work things out with her last partner. She knew she had a tendency to get judgmental and critical, and was just as afraid of hurting someone else as she was of getting hurt. With coaching, she broke those patterns and learned to communicate in clear, appreciative and affirming ways. Now she's dating someone she's excited about, but they're going slowly and checking in with us frequently to make sure they stay on course. Leila says, "I'm looking forward to spending the rest of my life loving consciously in a way I never could before. I wish I could have learned this stuff 50 years ago, but I'm so glad to learn it now. I finally feel equipped."

Cassandra, 75, was nervous she'd be our oldest client ever. (Actually, she isn't.) But she took our class anyway because "Learning how to have a healthy relationship is the one thing left to do in my life. I've done everything else I've wanted to do, but not that." In just the first few weeks, she reported that the class has been "revolutionary." She finally understands the communication patterns that wrecked her other relationships, and feels hopeful about love for the first time in a long time – though she says "I know I'm not ready for a relationship just yet. I have to become a Conscious Girlfriend first!"

Amy and Tanesha, 40 and 46, started coaching because they were fighting about everything and nothing, and in Tanesha's words, "We just can't take it any more. Love shouldn't be so hard." They also worried that their fighting was affecting Amy's two young children. In their first five sessions, they learned how to get to the root of their conflicts, stop bickering and punishing each other, and start re-building trust. Now they've recommitted to their relationship, and feel hopeful and excited about their love.

Sunny and Leza, 36 and 41, had a lot of self-awareness and communication skills already, yet their emotional triggers were wrecking their connection. Although they knew what the issues were, they kept getting stuck in blame, and felt bruised and hopeless. In just four coaching sessions they built new skills for getting through their triggers, and got their love back on track.

Whoever You Are, You Can Date Wisely and Love Well, Too

Although all of our clients are lesbians and queer women, they are very diverse in every other way. They come from all over the United States, and quite a few other countries, including the United Kingdom, Ireland, South Africa, the Philippines and Argentina. They range in age from 20 to 90. Really. And they come from every racial and cultural group, and every class background.

Some work in the corporate world, or are lawyers or physicians; others are self-employed craftswomen who make artisan soap, or professional astrologers. Some are old-time lesbian feminists; some are new-time queer women. We welcome lesbians, bisexual women, transwomen, queer women, butches, bois, studs, femmes, gay women, same-gender-loving women, dykes, and every other self-identified woman who loves women, or wants to.

Some have already had many relationships, or long relationships, and haven't been single much at all – while others have had few relationships and/or have been single for years or decades.

Some of our clients are in perfect health and completely able-bodied; others have serious health problems or disabilities. Some have histories of physical and/or sexual abuse. We understand. We do, too.

Regardless, there's one thing that's true for everyone we work with, and everyone reading these words – and that is that *being able to find the right partner and have a lasting, healthy, fulfilling relationship is an inside job.*

Whoever you are, and whatever your specific circumstances may be, you create your relationship life through your choices and actions. *You* are the one who determines whether or not you choose the right woman, and whether or not the relationship can be fulfilling and joyful.

No one can do it for you. But no one can stop you, either!

CHAPTER 2

Lesbian Relationships:
The Same & Different

In some ways, the challenges in lesbian relationships are the same as those in all other relationships. Yet in other ways, they're quite different. That's why Conscious Girlfriend incorporates cutting-edge scientific and psychological knowledge from the best relationship experts and researchers in the world – but also goes beyond their work, since those experts are all heterosexual and their work is largely focused on heterosexual couples.

Relationships between two women present very particular opportunities for deep intimacy, but also some dynamics that can derail us if we don't fully understand them or know how to handle them with skill. Both our work and our personal lives have shown us that lesbian relationships can be the deepest, most powerful relationships in the world – but they can also be the hardest, most painful relationships in the world, if you don't know how to navigate their specific challenges.

Because two women can bond so quickly and deeply, we often commit to one another very quickly. Problems arise when the woman with whom you've bonded, and to whom you've committed, is someone with whom you're not actually compatible.

Even once you recognize that someone isn't right for you, the level of emotional bonding often makes it very hard and painful for two women to separate. (We call this the "sticky lesbian super-glue" effect.)

Also, because of this same bonding, two women may emotionally trigger each other more intensely than other couples. Emotional triggers aren't rational; they don't mean there's anything wrong with us, and they're not our fault. Triggers are a product of our brain chemistry, part of the primitive "fight or flight" mechanism instilled in all of us in order to help us stay alive. Yet often when we're not actually facing mortal danger, our emotional triggers make our lives harder rather than easier.

All couples, of all orientations, emotionally trigger each other. It's just part of being human. Yet because lesbians have high expectations for emotional intimacy, we may run into these triggers even more often, and suffer even more from them. This can keep our relationships stuck in painful, unproductive loops.

All of these challenges are completely solvable, once you understand them and have the right skills. But if you don't, lesbian love can quickly take you from connection and bliss into excruciating pain.

Let's take a very personal look at how and why that can happen.

The Anatomy of a Lesbian Heartbreak

Ruth: *I was teaching at a writing conference when I first noticed Sarah across the room. As quickly as I could, I made a bee-line across the room to talk to her. I was thrilled when she suggested we have lunch together – and then again when she invited me over to her house that evening. There, my feelings grew even stronger when I saw that her bookshelves were lined with books by some of my favorite writers.*

The next day during our lunch hour, Sarah took me to a center that rehabilitated injured hawks. Since I love nature and have a particular passion for birds, it was the best date I could have ined. Later that afternoon, we took a walk in the woods, found a little shelter someone had made in the trees, and kissed for the first time. It was magic!

We saw each other again every day that week. On Friday night, Sarah finally invited me into her bed, and the passion between us was incredible. It looked and felt to me like the love I'd wanted all my life.

We had known each other for five days.

Does this story sound familiar? Perhaps you've lived out your own version of it, and if not, you've most likely seen friends do it. As the old joke says, "What does a lesbian bring on the second date? A U–Haul."

It wasn't until many years later that I learned that there is actually a name for this intense, rapid bonding phenomenon. Psychologists call it *limerence.*

When you're in limerence with someone, she looks perfect to you. You can't keep your hands off each other. You can't stop thinking about each other. It feels like love.

But it isn't.

Understanding Limerence

When you fall into limerence (which many of us call "falling in love,") it feels like you're high – and there's a good reason for that. You actually *are* high, stoned on endogenous opiates, your body's own version of heroin. When scientists do brain scans on people who are newly in love, they find massive quantities of these "feel-good" chemicals.

People of all genders and sexual orientations experience limerence – but in general, two women go into limerence more quickly and deeply than couples of other sexual orientations, and also move more rapidly into commitment. Many lesbians have sex have sex within the first few weeks of meeting, and then instantly begin a partnership. We've coached couples who met, got engaged and moved in together within three weeks.

In general, men seem to have a braking mechanism that keeps them from going into limerence as quickly, or moving straight from limerence into commitment. This explains why, on the whole, heterosexual and gay male relationships follow a very different pattern than lesbian relationships. After all, there's a reason why no one jokes about straight or gay male couples bringing a U-Haul on the second date!

In contrast, two women together are much more likely to go into intense, rapid limerence, interpret it as true love, and dive right in.

All human beings go into limerence, or get "high on love," because of our biology – specifically, the biological imperative to mate, reproduce and raise children. Even though two women can't create a child (at least, not without some help from a sperm donor), we're still governed by the same biochemistry.

Scientists theorize that nature created limerence in order to prod people to make babies and then stay together for long enough to get them out of infancy. Of course it doesn't always work out that way, since limerence can end within a few months, and it rarely lasts longer than a year. Our brains simply can't keep pumping out all those chemicals, and they're not supposed to.

But even when the limerence fades, lesbians tend to feel so bonded to one another that it's very hard to part. The deeper you've gone into limerence – and the more you've confused it with love – the more painful it is to separate. That's why lesbian break-ups can be the most shattering breakups on the planet.

The truth is, limerence isn't love – and unfortunately, it doesn't even necessarily lead to love. It can make two women feel intensely drawn to each other even when they're really not well-matched at all.

In fact, it often makes us skip over the process of even assessing whether we're truly right for each other – or leads us to ignore the signals that tell us we're not. That's what got me into big trouble.

Ruth: *Three months into my relationship with Sarah, she didn't call me one evening when she'd said she would. The next day, it turned out she'd been out drinking till 5 a.m. with one of her exes.*

I spent the whole day crying. I knew I should leave Sarah then, but I just couldn't. I was too deeply in love. So I stayed.

How Limerence Can Lead to Heartbreak

Limerence always wears off – usually within 3-6 months. Sometimes it lasts even less time, sometimes a little more. But it never lasts forever.

And it doesn't wear off at exactly the same moment for everyone. Often, one person emerges from limerence sooner than the other.

Limerence itself doesn't cause heartbreak. But when we confuse limerence with love, and make big life choices based on it, we set ourselves up for pain.

As we've discussed, limerence often leads us to choose partners with whom we're not actually compatible. Then, when the limerence wears off, one or both people may not be able to withstand the sudden jolt. Often this creates intense conflict, or even a breakup.

Ruth: *Ten months after we started our whirlwind romance, Sarah broke up with me suddenly and without explanation.*

I was devastated and in shock. I knew we'd had some big fights and painful times, but I thought we'd gotten through them. Or I thought we would get through them. I couldn't imagine my life without her.

I huddled for hours in the big green armchair in my living room, sobbing. I couldn't eat. I couldn't sleep. One night at 2 a.m. I actually called a suicide hotline. I wasn't really thinking about killing myself; I just couldn't figure out how to go on.

All breakups hurt, but breakups between two women can be worst of all, because we've often bonded so deeply. The emotional and even physical pain can be astonishingly intense. It can literally feel as if you're going to die.

This pain is a product of our hard-wired brain chemistry and the phenomenon psychologists call *attachment*. As infants, we *would* have died if our mother or other caretaker left us, and when we've bonded with a partner, that same primal attachment takes over.

Because of how deeply we bond, lesbians often go through more push-pull than other kinds of couples. We may break up and get back together again many times, making the pain and confusion even worse.

Ruth: *A month after Sarah broke up with me, we saw each other again and ended up in bed. I was thrilled.*

For the next three months, we spent every weekend together. Everything was pretty much as it had been before, except that Sarah insisted that we weren't back together. But it certainly felt as if we were. We made love a lot, and things between us were almost as wonderful as they had been in the beginning.

Then one day Sarah told me she was getting back together with her ex-partner. She acted as if I shouldn't have any feelings about that — since technically, according to her, we weren't together. Yet she seemed to have some feelings of her own. As she drove cross-country for their reunion, she called me three times to say how much she missed me.

I did my best to let go. I grieved hard.

But then a few months later, Sarah called and invited me to meet her at a hot springs resort in New Mexico.

Even though my head told me not to go, my heart leapt. And Sarah was pretty clear what her intentions were. "Do you think you'll still be attracted to me?" she asked, as if there was any doubt.

I bought my ticket and flew to meet her — but by the time she picked me up at the airport, she had changed her mind. She insisted I rent my own room, rather than staying with her. Then she spent hours on the phone changing her plane ticket so she could leave the next day.

It might be easy to see Sarah as the villain in this story. At least, that's how I saw it for quite a while. But in reality, I was just as responsible for my heartbreak as she was. The truth is, no one can break your heart without your participation.

On the other hand, maybe you're not seeing Sarah as a villain at all. Instead, you might be wondering why I was such a fool! That's a great question, because we work with women every single day who make the same kinds of bad choices I made, with the same painful results. Here's what we see:

When you've bonded deeply through limerence…

When you can see the other person's potential so clearly…

When you feel like there's a level of sexual, emotional and/or spiritual connection deeper than you've ever experienced before…

Or even just when she's the best prospect to come along in a long time, and you're afraid there won't be anyone else out there…

… It can be easy to ignore your wiser mind and set yourself up for pain the same way I did.

That's why Conscious Girlfriend's work focuses on teaching you how to pay attention to what you really need and who the other person really is, and then make choices that will lead to happiness rather than pain.

Sure, it's great to see her potential, and get excited about the potential you feel between you. But your potential can't have a relationship with her potential. You can only have a relationship with someone as she is right now – and as you are right now!

Of course, if you're both aware of problematic patterns you have right now, able to acknowledge them, and willing to consciously work toward changing them, you can both *live your way into your potential.*

It's a beautiful journey – but it won't happen without conscious, mutual effort.

After a heartbreak like the one I went through with Sarah, some lesbians stay single for years, even decades. Some never really let themselves fall in love again. Others go for the "hair of the dog" strategy, usually just creating more pain for themselves down the line. That's the path I chose.

Repeating the Cycle

Ruth: *A month after the disastrous hot-springs rendezvous with Sarah, I answered Leanne's personal ad. Deep down I knew I wasn't really ready for a new relationship, but I was hurting and lonely.*

Leanne looked perfect in a whole different way than Sarah had. She was a Buddhist with a daily meditation practice, and she had done seven years of therapy. She was also a great writer, funny, and loved to hike.

We zoomed straight into limerence. After our first date, we began writing each other several lengthy emails a day. We went to bed together on our second date a week later, and then became an instant couple.

It turned out to be the hardest relationship of my life.

When you're in limerence with someone, you feel so blissed-out and connected that your relationship feels "meant to be."

Even if part of your mind can recognize potential (or definite) problem areas between you, the *feeling* of rightness is likely to be overpowering.

Even if your friends don't like her. Even if you start having little or big arguments early on. Even if she mistreats you. Even if you can see that she drinks too much, or notice other "red flags." Even if your communication starts going terribly awry… limerence can talk you out of doing what you know is best.

We've found that most of the single women we work with saw red flags early on in their relationships, but they didn't let themselves pay full attention to what they were observing. Instead, they told themselves things like this:

"Well, nobody's perfect. Who am I to judge?"

"I want to give her the benefit of the doubt."

"It'll change once we get to know each other better."

"She's the best one to come along in a long time. There's probably no one better out there."

"We'll be able to work it out."

"I'm already in too deep to pull out now. It would hurt too much. Or, it would hurt *her* too much."

I understand. I used to say these things, too.

But the bottom line is, if you want a happy, healthy lasting relationship, you need to learn how to choose a partner wisely. And although limerence is powerful, it's not wise.

Breaking the Cycle

If you've read this far, we're guessing it's because you're ready to break the cycle and learn a different way to date and love, a way that will actually bring you lasting happiness. If so, we're delighted to walk you through the 12-Week Roadmap to Conscious Lesbian Dating & Lasting Love.

We offer the 12-Week Roadmap as an online course to women all over the world, and since it comes with an abundance of audio lessons, worksheets, exercises, and live coaching calls, we won't be able to fully replicate the whole experience here. But in this book, we'll give you as much of the Roadmap as we can.

CHAPTER 3

Why the 12-Week Roadmap to Conscious Lesbian Dating & Lasting Love?

Our students regularly tell us that the 12-Week Roadmap course gives them huge "aha" or "eureka" moments, insights they've never gotten elsewhere. Even if you've been in therapy, spent years meditating, or done a lot of other personal growth work, you may not have gotten the dating or relationship help you needed – both because intimate relationships are the final frontier for most of us, and because most healing modalities don't take into account the particular dynamics of love between women.

The 12-Week Roadmap covers the skills involved in two separate, though related, skill-sets: the conscious dating process, and the process of creating and maintaining a happy, healthy relationship. We've found that lesbians and queer women need to be well-grounded in *both* areas in order to find a truly compatible partner and then build a solid, fulfilling relationship.

As we've said before, in order to have the kind of lasting love you want, you need to do two things: find the right partner, and learn how to *be* the right partner. The Roadmap will teach you both.

You'll learn how to date and what to look for when you date, how to be clear on your relationship vision and stick to it, how to listen to your gut and brain as well as your heart and chemistry, and how to choose a partner wisely.

And you'll also learn the skills you'll need to create a deeply fulfilling love relationship with your new partner – and keep it that way.

We spend the first six weeks of the 12-Week Roadmap on the relationship skills – *being* the right partner – because you won't be able to meet the right woman until you're truly ready for her. (Actually, no one can really *be* the right woman until you're ready.)

So, the first half of the Roadmap will help you:

- **Understand what a healthy relationship really is** – and also identify the unhealthy beliefs about relationships that you may still be holding somewhere inside yourself, like "True love is about sacrifice," or "I'll always have to give more than the other person does."

- **Develop a healthy, solid foundation of self-love** and self-compassion, and release patterns of treating yourself harshly or criticizing yourself.

- **Guide you through the process of making peace with your past relationships,** recognizing the part you played in co-creating them (even if it was only by choosing the wrong woman and/or staying too long), and forgiving yourself.

- **Develop the ability to recognize and befriend your own emotions** – which is key to being able to share your feelings with a partner in a healthy, intimacy-building way.

- **Learn the secrets of great communication**, so you can avoid the vast majority of conflicts, fights, misunderstandings and hurt feelings *before they even start.*

- **Build your skill at using our #1 conflict-resolving tool**, the SCORE process, so that when conflicts *do* get going, you can easily stop them and heal them at their root, rather than having the same fight over and over again.

This process really works! In just six weeks, we've seen women go from feeling cynical and hopeless about relationships – or about their ability to ever create the kind of relationship they want – to feeling energized, inspired, hopeful and confident. And that confidence and inspiration isn't empty or misplaced. It's based on *finally knowing what to do.*

Look at it this way: if you really wanted to drive across the country, but you didn't know how to operate a car – and you didn't know how or where to learn – it would feel pretty intimidating, maybe even hopeless. But once you'd had some intensive driving lessons, you could plan for your road-trip with excitement. And it wouldn't be magical thinking or fantasy – it would be excitement based in reality, because you'd know you had the driving skills to make the trip.

Michelle: *Between Ruth and I, there are faint echoes of the patterns that destroyed our previous relationships – but we know how to work with them now, so they don't get in our way. But if we'd met five or ten years earlier – wow. I don't even want to think about it. We'd have been a disaster.*

In the second six weeks of the 12-Week Roadmap, we focus on dating skills – the nuts and bolts (and also the deeper stuff) involved in finding women to date, assessing each woman you date to see whether she's right for you, and then actually finding *her.*

In this part of the process, we help you:

- **Develop somatic (body-based) skills to help you overcome your fears** about dating and relationships. Fear often blocks us from even attempting the things we most want to do, but it doesn't have to. Yet it doesn't work well to try to talk yourself out of your fears, because many of them are held in your body, not your mind. That's why body-based tools are so important in getting you through them.

- **Understand the truth (and bust the myths) about attraction, chemistry and compatibility.** Although attraction and chemistry are important aspects of lasting love, we find that many women are focusing on them in ways that just don't work. We teach you about what attraction means and doesn't, how it can change, and about the three levels of compatibility. We've found that Level 3, which isn't on most peoples' radar, is actually the #1 factor in being able to sustain a happy, healthy relationship.

- **Craft your vision for your ideal relationship.** Although all good relationships share certain features – like compassion, emotional self-responsibility, good communication and the ability to resolve conflicts with love and respect – each one is also a unique co-creation of the two people in it. And if you don't have a crystal-clear understanding of exactly what you want, you're not very likely to create it. That's why we lead you through a process of discovering and defining that vision for yourself – so when someone who might be Ms. Right shows up, it's easy to find out whether you and she are actually looking for the same things (and avoid a huge potential heartbreak if you're not.)

- **Develop an effective dating plan** that fits your personality and circumstance. We're big fans of online dating, because it widens the pool so much, but there are big pitfalls to watch out for, too. We'll help you learn exactly what works and what doesn't in online dating – or help you identify the best local ways to meet women, if you'd rather go that route. Either way, dating with a plan and a strategy works a whole lot better than trying to date without one.

- **Learn how to handle lust, limerence and infatuation.** We'll teach you how to proceed wisely even when limerence strikes, so you can find out more about the woman who's made your brain chemistry go haywire. When you know how, you can enjoy the fun of the ride without risking your heart.

- **Understand how to truly assess your compatibility** with the women you date, without feeling like you're awkwardly interviewing them – or giving them "the benefit of the doubt" and setting yourself up for pain.

- **Gracefully end the dating process** if you realize the woman you've been seeing is not a good potential match for you – or consciously deepen it, but only if and when your body, brain, heart and gut all agree.

Again, we cover relationship skills in the first six weeks and dating skills in the second, because we've found that having a good grasp of communication and conflict-healing skills is actually a prerequisite to successful dating.

There are a few reasons for this. One is that misunderstandings, communication glitches and emotional triggers often come up even in the first few dates with someone – so if you're not prepared to handle those with skill, a great potential relationship could be dead in the water.

But we've also found that on some level, we all know it when we don't have all the skills we need. Even if you're not aware of it, you're likely to respond to your unreadiness by blocking yourself from going full-force toward the kind of passionate, deeply connected relationship you really want.

Think about it. Why would you want to fall deeply in love with a truly compatible partner, only to mess things up by not being able to ask for what you need, say what you feel, listen to what *she* needs and feels, and heal whatever conflicts come up? It would be so painful and frustrating to find the love of your life and then not be able to make things work.

And so most of us don't. We keep ourselves from finding her – or from recognizing that we've found her – until we're fully prepared to create lasting love.

Why Women Stay Single

Most of the single women who work with us believe they're single because they just haven't met the right woman.

Maybe you date, but nothing seems to click; you meet women, but there's no spark, and the connection just doesn't go deeper.

Or maybe you're not sure how to start dating. Either you don't know how to meet women, or you don't know how to ask them out. You might wonder how to turn an acquaintance or friend into a potential dating partner, or even whether that's a good idea.

You might also have been in and out of painful relationships so many times that you feel doubtful about the possibility of healthy love. A lot of the women who come to us feel that way. And we've certainly been there, too.

"I'm always attracted to the wrong women," our student Lara told us cheerfully, though her smile didn't really hide her pain. "I've gotten to the point where if I'm attracted to someone, I know she'll be bad for me. So why try?"

Other women express more hope. We often hear, "I just have to meet the right woman." Yet there's a sense of confusion and doubt beneath those words – because if she's really out there, how come you haven't met her yet, and what will it take to find her?

Through working with hundreds of women, we've learned several things.

- **She *is* out there.** Many thousands of lesbians and queer women of all ages, races and physical types want happy, healthy, lasting love (and are willing to do the work to create it!) So whoever you are, if that's your dream, there is someone who wants to find you just as much as you want to find her.

- **You won't be able to find her until you're truly ready for her.** Until then, your search will be an exercise in frustration – because you either won't recognize Ms. Right, you'll be involved with another Ms. Wrong by the time she shows up, or you won't have the know-how to work through whatever challenges come up and create a strong, lasting relationship her.

Why You Need To Be Ready Before She Shows Up

Some women think, "Well, I'll find her first – and then we'll figure it out." But the truth is, it actually wouldn't go very well if you met Ms. Right before you were ready for her.

In my previous relationships, when things went wrong, I had a tendency to blame my partners – and in Michelle's previous relationships, she always blamed herself. It's easy to see how my patterns and hers would have fit together like a lock and key – a painful key, in a dysfunctional lock.

If we'd met before we had the skills to consciously work with and overcome those patterns, we would just have created a big mess of pain and confusion. We would have tried our best to love each other, failed, broken up, and licked our wounds – without ever even understanding what had happened.

And that's actually what we both experienced when our other relationships ended – even though each one had its own problematic patterns, and ended for its own reasons.

In fact, in a way the reasons for those "failed" relationships (we like to put the word "failed" in quotes, because after all, we did learn things – even though the process was a lot more painful than it needed to be), was always the same:

We didn't know how to choose the right woman, and we also didn't know how to navigate love's challenges and keep it strong.

Now, we *do* know how to do those things – and we're here to teach you, too. Once you have a "roadmap" for lasting love, and you know how to navigate the twists and turns of the road, you too can find and create a truly happy, healthy lasting love.

If You Don't Feel Ready

If you don't feel ready for another relationship, that's great. We love it when women tell us, "I'm not ready," because it means you're paying attention.

Of course, another part of the truth is that it's hard to really be ready until you've got a roadmap. Who'd want to set off on a cross-country trip without one?

(Well, these days you could just use a GPS or navigation system. Maybe someday we'll create an automated version of this course, so that when conflict or questions arise, you can just push a button and hear an automated voice tell you what to do! But we're not quite there yet.)

We are huge supporters of women not dating until they're really ready for a new relationship – because we've seen so many women who knew they weren't ready "test the dating waters" anyway, and get into big trouble.

Connie's Dating-Too-Soon Story

Connie, 46, had ended a long-term relationship a year before, and didn't feel ready for another partner – but she thought she'd just date a little bit and have some fun.

Unfortunately, it didn't work out that way. First, two women she was casually dating both fell in love with her, and put a lot of pressure on her to get involved with them. (The sad truth is that for many women, someone who's not fully available is a powerful magnetic force.)

Then, even though Connie managed to avoid getting into either of those relationships, she ended up falling head-over-heels for someone else. In the grip of strong emotion, she decided to go for it, and you can guess what happened: a very painful, confusing breakup, just a few months down the line.

Connie's story did have a happy ending, though, because she ended up going through our program, healing her heart, and truly getting ready for love. Last we heard, she was dating a wonderful woman in a truly sane way, rather than blindly diving in the way she had so many times before.

Here's an overview of the entire 12-Week Roadmap, step by step. We've included "landmarks" – the skills or abilities you'll have once you've completed each week's work.

Overview: The 12-Week Roadmap to Conscious Lesbian Dating & Lasting Love

PART ONE:
Prepare Your Heart & Mind for the Relationship You Want

Week 1: Understand What a Healthy Relationship Is – And Open To It

- ✓ Learn and explore the key qualities of a conscious, healthy relationship, so you know where you're headed.
- ✓ Identify and release old beliefs that no longer serve you.

Landmark: *Once you've completed this week's step, you'll be clearer about the healthy relationship you want, and more fully open to it.*

Week 2: Eliminate Self-Criticism & Build Self-Compassion & Self-Love

- ✓ Transform your inner critic into an inner advocate, and make self-compassion your automatic "go-to" response.

Landmark: *Once you've completed this week's step, you'll become more able to love yourself – which will help you give love to others, and receive their love more fully.*

Week 3: Complete Your Unfinished Business

- ✓ Come to terms with what really happened between you and your ex-partner(s) – and how you co-created it. Then, *forgive yourself.*

Landmark: *Once you've completed this week's step, you'll be at peace with the past, and open to creating a whole new future.*

Week 4: Know & Befriend Your Own Emotions

✓ Develop the ability to know what you feel when you feel it – and become able to welcome your emotions, rather than being controlled by them.

Landmark: *Once you've completed this week's step, you'll be far more comfortable and intimate with yourself, and better able to sustain intimacy with others.*

Week 5: Speak & Listen To Build Intimacy

✓ Learn how to speak and listen cleanly and in ways that keep connection strong (and zap your unconscious intimacy-killing habits.)

Landmark: *Once you've completed this week's step, you'll have the skills to communicate openly, easily and effectively, in ways that build connection.*

Week 6: Gain & Practice the Skills Involved In Healing Conflict

✓ Bring all the previous weeks' learning together in the SCORE Process, a groundbreaking way to dismantle triggers, stop fighting and resolve conflict at its source.

Landmark: *Once you've completed this week's step, you'll be done with fighting and hours of draining 'processing.' Even when there is conflict, you'll be able to heal your triggers and stay close to yourself and others.*

PART TWO:
Successful Dating – Here's How To Find Her.

<u>Week 7: Overcome Dating- and Relationship-Related Fears & Blocks</u>

- ✓ Learn powerful body-based techniques for transforming fear – and heal your fear of rejection, fear of hurting someone or being hurt, and other dating fears.

  Landmark: *Once you've completed this week's step, you'll feel ready to meet women and date with confidence and an open heart.*

<u>Week 8: Learn the Truth (And Bust the Myths) About Attraction, Chemistry & Compatibility</u>

- ✓ Understand what kinds of chemistry, attraction and compatibility are truly necessary.

  Landmark: *Once you've completed this week's step, you'll know exactly what to look for – and what to avoid – in a potential partner.*

<u>Week 9: Create Your Relationship Vision</u>

- ✓ Design your ideal relationship, and get crystal-clear on what it offers and requires.

  Landmark: *Once you've completed this week's step, you'll be clear on your must-haves and deal-breakers, so you can quickly recognize who's right and who's not – and stick to your vision.*

<u>Week 10: Develop Your Dating Plan</u>

   ✓ Explore the online and in-person options for meeting women, and the advantages and pitfalls of each method – and then chart your dating course.

Landmark: *Once you've completed this week's step, you'll have a dating plan that's effective and smart for your heart.*

<u>Week 11: Outsmart Your Hardwired Brain Chemistry.</u>

   ✓ Recognize the difference between limerence and love, and make good choices even when smitten by lust or infatuation.

Landmark: *Once you've completed this week's step, you'll be able to keep your body, brain and heart on the same conscious page.*

<u>Week 12: Date, Communicate & Assess (And Rinse, Lather, Repeat.)</u>

   ✓ Skillfully navigate the first few dates, gracefully stop dating someone when necessary, and/or consciously deepen the connection when you choose.

Landmark: *Once you've completed this week's step, you'll be in the "dating driver's seat" – and you'll be a great driver.*

What You Can Learn In Just 12 Weeks

Yes, we know – that's a lot to cover.

We created this course to help women develop a lot of very important skills in a very short time frame. In other words, we don't want to just give you a fish or two – we want to teach you to fish, help you choose the right fishing pole, help you find the right waters to cast it into, and then also make sure you know what to do when you feel that exciting tug on your fishing line.

But we know that this outline might seem overwhelming. "Whoa. Can I really master all of that? And won't it take me years?"

No, it won't. And yes, it will. Both statements are true at once. Let us explain.

Some of the practices in the Roadmap involve skills you could certainly continue to hone for a lifetime. Most of us can always get better at communicating clearly, listening well, and dismantling our triggers to prevent conflict from taking hold.

We can also spend the rest of our lives improving our ability to fully love ourselves, stop criticizing ourselves, and respond to our feelings with compassion. And, it's always possible to reach deeper and deeper levels of peace about what's happened in the past – and open our hearts even further to the present moment.

Yet at the same time, although we can spend decades getting better and better at all of the above – and that's a very worthwhile endeavor that will richly reward us in happiness and well-being – it's also possible to make huge strides in those directions within a very short time.

Let us give you an example:

If you've never ridden a bicycle, you can learn how to ride one in a matter of hours or days – and the difference between "life before being able to ride a bike" and "life once you know how to ride a bike" will be *huge*. You'll be able to hop on the bike and tool around the block, make a quick run to the store, enjoy the breeze, coast down the hill, and get a great cardio workout pedaling back up.

Is there still room for you to become a better cyclist? Of course. Pro cyclists train for years. Yet once you know how to ride a bicycle, you'll always know how to ride one. The body never forgets. The skills you've gained will stay with you forever.

And if you've ever experienced the difference between walking and pedaling somewhere, you know how much easier your life can be when you can ride, rather than walk.

Acquiring relationship skills is similar. Although you can spend the rest of your life getting better and better at them, your relationship life will change dramatically just from getting a basic level of know-how – and that, you can definitely achieve in 12 weeks.

In fact, you can begin the process of getting those skills in the next hour or two, as you read this book. You probably won't learn them as fully as you would if we were coaching you, leading you through exercises, and guiding you – just as you couldn't learn to play tennis as well from a book as from having a coach who stood behind you and physically moved your arms to adjust your serve. Yet you could still pick up a great deal just from reading about how to play tennis – and you can also learn a lot from reading about the 12-Week Roadmap to Conscious Lesbian Dating & Lasting Love.

In the chapters that follow, we'll take you through the entire Roadmap, so you can begin to experience the insights – and the healing and inspiring possibilities – for yourself.

CHAPTER 4

Getting Started On the 12-Week Roadmap

Your Commitment to Yourself

We want to start by congratulating you for taking this step and beginning this journey. And since we know you may be feeling nervous, we suggest that you start by giving yourself a big pat on the back and a lot of appreciation for making the effort to find out how to date wisely and create a happy, healthy relationship.

The Roadmap is designed to give you the guidance and support that you need to understand your emotional patterns, where you may have gone wrong in relationships in the past, and how you can make whatever changes you need to make so that you can have the love life you really want.

When we teach and coach women, we do everything in our power to create a loving, safe, supportive container – and even though it's hard to do the same thing with words on a page, we're going to give it our best shot.

Now, here's what we need from you:

To date wisely and create a happy relationship, you have to be aware of your feelings – so we suggest that you notice what you're feeling and what's coming up for you, as you read each page of this book.

In fact, we encourage this to be the first commitment you make in this new phase of your journey toward the love you want: *the commitment to pay close attention to yourself and your feelings, and also notice what you do with those feelings.*

For instance, you might notice that you're feeling emotional, or that fear is bubbling up inside you – perhaps in the form of a knot in your stomach, tight shoulders, or a sore spot in your heart.

If that's happening, you might also notice yourself trying to push away that fear, or talk yourself out of it. Fear is a common and challenging feeling for most of us, so we'll be going into a lot more detail about how to work with it – but for now, just let yourself observe it.

Or, you might find that you're not feeling very much at all – that you're just engaging with this book mentally, not emotionally. Or you might feel cranky, or frustrated, or impatient, or excited.

Whatever you're feeling or not feeling is fine. There's no right or wrong. What's important is that you *notice* what you're feeling – and ideally, to notice it without judging it. That's one of the most important steps you can take on this road to the happy, healthy relationship you want.

How to Use This Book

We suggest that you use a special notebook or journal to do the exercises in this book, and also just note your thoughts, feelings and questions as they come up.

If at any point you want some support directly from us, you can also email us to set up some coaching, or join one of our online Roadmap classes.

We also encourage you to give yourself the space to make mistakes as you begin putting the practices we describe into action – and to let yourself feel scared, uncertain, sad or angry as you work through the lessons. That's all part of the process of learning new skills. You can't really learn much unless you're willing to stretch in some new directions, and to love yourself through that process.

Michelle: *I had many negative tapes running in my mind for many years, about who I was and why I hadn't found the right person to love. The truth is, the most important person for me to love was myself. That was a huge piece of the puzzle for me, and I've found that that's true for many women.*

We're going to be teaching you more about how to create more self-love very soon. But for now, let's start by defining what a healthy relationship really is.

Roadmap Week One

Understand What A Healthy Relationship Is – And Open To It

Here's the Conscious Girlfriend definition of a healthy relationship.

A healthy intimate relationship takes place between two adults who:

- Are able to feel compassionate for themselves and each other.

- Are self-aware enough to know what they feel, when they feel it.

re able to tolerate their own emotions without exploding, tacking, shutting down, withdrawing or self-medicating.

- Are able and willing to communicate their feelings without blaming themselves or each other.

- And, are whole-heartedly willing to learn and grow.

We've come up with a quick way for you to remember all that. We call it C.A.T.C.H., so that when you're looking for a woman who's a "good catch," you know exactly what that is.

So here are those qualities again, in abbreviated form. To have a happy, healthy relationship, you need to find a woman with the following qualities and abilities:

C = Compassion toward herself and toward you

A = Aware (self-aware) enough to know what she feels when she feels it.

T = Tolerates her own emotions without exploding, attacking, shutting down, withdrawing or self-medicating.

C = Communicates her feelings without blaming herself or you.

H = (Whole)Heartedly willing to learn and grow.

And of course, you not only need to find a woman who has those qualities – you need to *be* a woman who has those qualities, too. So, to be a "catch" yourself – and to be able to have the lasting, happy, healthy love you want – you need to have:

C = Compassion toward yourself, as well as others.

A = Awareness of what you feel, when you feel it.

T = (The ability to) Tolerate your own emotions without exploding, attacking, shutting down, withdrawing or self-medicating.

C = (The ability to) Communicate your feelings without blaming yourself or anyone else.

H = (w)hole-Heartedly willingness to learn and grow.

When Two "Catches" Find Each Other

We're not saying that everything is always easy when two women who are each a "catch" in this way get together. There are always communication glitches and different needs to work through. There are also all the various kinds of challenges life throws at us — issues like work, parenting, health issues, money problems, schedule challenges, family troubles, and everything else people deal with.

But if you're both "catches," there won't be drama. There won't be bickering, fights, nastiness, lying, deception or cruelty. Ever.

And when there's no drama, bickering, fights, nastiness, lying, deception or cruelty, there is room for joy, connection, ease, and intimacy.

That's the joy of a healthy relationship!

We can tell you that for sure, because we live this every day. Since getting together 9+ years ago now, we've been through cross-country moves, economic challenges, career changes, serious health issues, family crises and more. Yet even when things are rough, and even when we get triggered or scared, we manage to communicate with love and respect.

There are tears sometimes, for sure. But there's also plenty of laughter.

One of the things we love most about our relationship is that it gives us the gift of feeling seen, heard, accepted and loved just the way we are — *and* also supports us in growing and changing.

We all need both. We want and need to be loved as we are – since it's not possible to be loved as we are not! (And it certainly wouldn't feel good to have someone say, "I love your potential, but not who you are right now.")

But we also need space to grow and change, because growth is a constant for human beings, just as it is for everything else alive.

Ruth: *Michelle and I had a great relationship before, but since we started Conscious Girlfriend, we've upped the ante. Because we spend all our time talking, thinking and writing about relationship skills, we use them even more fully than we did before. And because we have different personalities and abilities, there are always more things to learn and work out. It's a good thing we know how to enjoy the process!*

Identifying Your Beliefs about Relationships

Now that you know what a healthy relationship really is, let's take a look at what you may have previously believed about relationships – because chances are, those beliefs are still operating somewhere inside you.

And you won't be able to change those beliefs until you know what they are.

Michelle: *For many years, I had three major beliefs about relationships:*

1. *Real love lasts forever.*

2. *Real love means giving myself up.*

3. *I have to give my partner more than she gives me, because otherwise she won't love me.*

In my first long-term relationship I played out all of these beliefs. I promised to stay forever, I gave myself up completely, and I gave much, much more than my partner Mary did.

But in the end, in order to be true to myself, I had to break my promise to be with Mary forever, and then I had to develop some new beliefs. Otherwise, I could never have found – or tolerated – the happy, healthy relationship Ruth and I share today.

Now we invite you to take a look at some of *your* beliefs about relationships. We'll start you off with a few of the negative beliefs we've heard from the women we coach:

- Relationships mean suffering and hard work.

- Marriage is a commitment you make to God. Your own desires are irrelevant.

- Marriage means your life is over. Whatever dreams or plans you had, you can no longer pursue them, because you're not living for yourself any more, you're living for the other person.

- Sex won't last in a long-term lesbian relationship.

- My relationship won't last unless I compromise more than she does.

- I need to censor myself in my relationships, because if I'm too honest, the other person will run away.

- Lesbian relationships are always unstable and full of drama.

Whoa, that's quite a list. If all – or even any – of those beliefs were really true, who in her right mind would even *want* a relationship?

Yet the interesting thing is that alongside these kinds of unconscious or only half-conscious negative beliefs, most of us also hold some impossibly-positive beliefs about relationships (another word for an impossibly-positive belief is "fantasy.") The surprising thing is that we can believe both extremely bleak beliefs, and completely rose-colored beliefs, at the very same time, even though they contradict each other.

Common impossibly-positive beliefs or fantasies include:

- Love means your problems are over. Once you find love, you'll never feel hurt or lonely again; you'll always be happy.

- When you're with the right person, everything will be easy.

- Marriage will fulfill all your needs.

- If it's true love, your partner will automatically know what you feel and want. She'll be able to read your mind.

- Love means a constant stream of sexual passion and bliss. You both automatically know exactly what to do to please each other sexually, you want all the same things with the same frequency, and you have simultaneous multiple orgasms every time you make love.

Wow – if we believe all or even any of those things, no wonder we want relationships!

Yet no wonder our real-life relationships can feel so bitterly disappointing, frustrating, confusing and painful – since every one of those beliefs is entirely unrealistic.

Now, take some time to explore inside yourself, and write down whatever beliefs you find you hold about relationships. Do your best to search through your mental and emotional inventory of images about love, and write down whatever you find or sense there – even if you already know it really isn't true, or know that you cognitively disagree with it.

Practice: *Make a list of your negative beliefs about relationships.*

Women sometimes have a hard time identifying their semi-conscious beliefs. One way to do it is simply by looking closely at any ideas or thoughts that make you feel discouraged, scared or pessimistic about relationships. Underneath each one, you'll find a belief.

For instance, if you find yourself thinking, "This all sounds good, but it won't work for me," that's a belief.

Or if you think, "There's no one out there to whom I'd be attracted, who would also be attracted to me *and* who would want to take a conscious approach to relationships" – that's a belief, too.

If you're aware of beliefs that were taught to you as a kid, or that your parents held, write them down too, even if you think you don't hold them – because they may still be in there influencing you somehow. You can also write down the circumstances that led you to develop the beliefs.

Ruth: *My father used to rage at my mother, "I feel like a slave under the whip!" He was the breadwinner, and he was always upset at her for spending too much money. I probably formed various different beliefs from that experience, but the one I seem to hold most strongly is that "It would never be safe for me to financially support someone else, or be supported by someone else."*

Now, as an adult I have always chosen to remain financially independent from my partners, and that's a valid choice to make. But when I really look at the issue, I see that underneath my valid adult choice, there's still the fear of a child.

Of course, you can inquire into whatever ideas and thoughts you have that make you feel encouraged, excited or optimistic about relationships, too. Those are based on beliefs, as well – so you can check them out to make sure they're realistic positive beliefs, rather than unrealistic fantasies.

Practice: *Make a list of your unrealistically-positive beliefs (fantasies) about relationships.*

After Identifying Your Beliefs

Once you've written both your lists, take a little while to sit with both of them. Let the knowledge sink in: *This is what's been running my relationship life from underneath.*

Allow yourself to notice whatever feelings come up, and remind yourself to try to feel compassion.

After all, if you're like most of us, you've probably been carrying around some impossibly contradictory beliefs – some of which made you want to run away from relationships in order to preserve your well-being, others of which made you think of relationships as the answer to every struggle you've ever had.

Our client Maria had been trying for years to find a partner, but none of her attempts at dating ever went very far. When she did this exercise, she realized that deep down, she believed that any relationship would be a life-or-death power struggle. That was what she'd witnessed between her parents. No wonder she'd kept herself single!

We live in a culture that's pretty confused about relationships. Hollywood and pop music certainly show us both the "angel" and "demon" versions of love, though they don't tell us much about how to get to the first one, or avoid the second. And you may have grown up with parents who held both kinds of views – perhaps espousing one view and living out another.

Once you've taken time to sit with your feelings, we'd like to suggest that you do two radical things.

Practice: *Shifting Your Beliefs*

First, read through your list and identify the beliefs you would like to get rid of – to burn up in an imaginary fire.

Then *build that fire inside your mind, and burn them.*

Or you can actually do this process physically:

1. Cut or tear your list of beliefs so that each belief you want to burn is on a separate little piece of paper.
2. Now, light a candle – or a fire in your fireplace, if you have one – and feed each belief you're ready to get rid of into the flames.

(Do be mindful of your physical safety while doing this, of course. And don't pour any gasoline onto those flames.)

But… watch those beliefs burn. Watch the fire eat them up, leaving only a little bit of ash in their place.

Now, notice what you feel. How does it feel in your body to burn those beliefs? How does it feel in your heart? Was there any part of you that wanted to hold onto any of them (or maybe even *did* hold onto some of them?)

If so, that's fine. This process is about noticing what you feel – not judging or forcing yourself. As the great gay poet Walt Whitman said, "So I contradict myself? Very well then, I contradict myself. I am large. I contain multitudes."

You, too, contradict yourself and contain multitudes. It's great to identify beliefs you're ready to get rid of, and then mentally or physically burn them up.

Is it really that simple to get rid of long-held beliefs? Yes and no. Symbolic rituals can be surprisingly powerful as a way of embodying your new awareness and intention. But of course, it's also just part of a larger process.

And a big part of the power comes from simply becoming aware of the beliefs you've been holding. Once you bring it your conscious awareness, it loses much of its unconscious power.

Sometimes, when we first become aware of a negative belief or a fantasy, we don't feel ready to give it up. That's fine. Just let yourself notice all your feelings about it. In a month or two, you can take another look at your list, and see whether it still feels the same to you, or whether anything has changed. Then you can choose what you want to keep, what you want to tweak, and what you want to let go of.

You might also find you hold some beliefs that you're not sure about. Are they healthy, or not? For instance, our coaching client Jennifer uncovered the belief that "Love requires large doses of forgiveness and tenderness." At first that sounded good to her, but then she thought, "Wait, does that mean I'm assuming my partner will do things I have to forgive? What if she doesn't do anything wrong?"

If you want, you can even sort your beliefs into four piles:

Beliefs I Want To Burn

Beliefs I'm Not Ready to Let Go of Yet – Though I May Get There

Beliefs I'm Not Sure About

Beliefs I Agree With and Want to Keep

Beliefs You Want to Keep

So, what beliefs would you want to keep? Let's take a look at those. These might be beliefs you've worked hard on developing, or acquired later in life. Or if you're lucky enough to have grown up around a good relationship, that undoubtedly shaped your beliefs too.

For instance, our coaching client Zena grew up with parents who were truly loving and respectful of each other. So she uncovered a belief that "True love means loving and respecting your partner," which she certainly wanted to keep. But she also realized she needed to choose her partners more wisely, because she'd been repeatedly hurt by women who didn't know how to love as well as her parents had loved each other.

Perhaps you haven't yet had any beliefs you really want to In that case, it's time to develop some! Yes, you can choose the beliefs you want to create and cultivate – and we recommend that you choose beliefs that really line up with the kind of relationship you want.

Sometimes women say, "I don't even know *what* to believe. I've never seen or been in a really happy, healthy relationship, so I don't know what it takes."

If that's the case for you, this process will be a great process of discovery. You can make a study, both inside yourself (studying your own thoughts, feelings and images) and outside yourself (studying the relationships of everyone you know, and even the relationships of people you hear or read about) and ask yourself, "Hmm, what's unhealthy here, and what's healthy? What are the qualities of the relationship I'd really want to be in, and what are things I'd want to make sure to avoid?"

Here are some of the new beliefs our coaching clients have come up with:

- My partner and I genuinely have each other's best interests at heart.

- I can pay attention to my own heart and well-being while I'm in a relationship.

- Love gives you strength, even (or especially) in tough times.

- My partner and I try our best to meet each other's sexual needs.

- Love means actively supporting your partner's outside interests and friendships.

- My partner and I are both be able and willing to see our own part in whatever is happening, and take full responsibility for it.

- Love means accepting and appreciating our differences.

- We'll be able to communicate without blaming each other.

- We'll show up and have the hard conversations when we need to. (*Our suggestion in response to this belief was, "Perhaps those conversations won't even have to be hard!"*)

Now, we invite you to make your own list of beliefs you already have, that you want to keep – and/or beliefs you don't yet hold, that you want to cultivate. These beliefs will help you get a clear, embodied sense of the kind of relationship you deeply want.

Practice: *Make your list of realistically-positive relationship beliefs now.*

Even though this list is intended to be realistic, not based on fantasy, some of what you write down may seem so different from your past experience that you find you have trouble believing it. If that happens, don't worry about it. Just let yourself notice that disbelief, and acknowledge it with compassion. As you work through the rest of the Roadmap, we predict that these healthy relationship beliefs will become easier and easier to hold.

You might also notice some fear coming up – and again, if that happens, just do your best to acknowledge it with compassion. Later on in the Roadmap, you'll get a chance to work with your fear more actively.

We do have one belief that we'd like to suggest you adopt. Here it is:

If I develop the right skills and choose the right partner, we can have a deeply satisfying, happy, healthy relationship. And, neither of us will be perfect, we will both trigger each other, and we'll need to keep using our skills to work through whatever comes up in an atmosphere of respect and love.

Yes, we know it may not sound romantic when we put it that way. But the truth is, our imperfect, deeply satisfying, happy, healthy relationship is very romantic! And yours can be, too.

Opening To the Relationship You Want

Now, let yourself begin to imagine that you can actually have a relationship that matches your most realistically-positive beliefs. Let yourself begin to want this relationship. Tell yourself that she is out there, and that you deserve her. See if you feel able to hold the intention of opening up to this image of happy, healthy love, even if you're not yet sure how you'll find it.

Notice what you feel in your body. Is there a sense of loosening and ease? Is there a sense of clenching, tightening or pushing away? You might feel either of those things, or even both of them at once. You might feel warmth, or coolness, aching or burning – or something else.

Remember, whatever you feel is okay. Don't push yourself – just invite, allow, and observe. It's all useful information that will help you on your journey.

If you do notice parts of yourself that are not yet fully open to this new vision, that's perfectly normal. After all, this is only Week #1 of the 12-Week Roadmap. The next 11 weeks will help you get the rest of the way there.

CHAPTER 5

Roadmap Week Two: Eliminate Your Self-Criticism and Build Self-Compassion & Self-Love

Some of our coaching clients feel they don't want to spend time on self-love, since what they're really hoping for is love from someone else. We sometimes hear, "I'm tired of having to do everything for myself. Isn't it okay to want to receive from someone else instead?"

And our answer to that is: Of course! Yet there is a crucial connection between loving yourself, and being loved by someone else. We've actually found that building your self-love and self-compassion is a key part of becoming able to get more love from others, including a wonderful partner.

So let's take a closer look at self-compassion and self-love. They're both important, and they're closely related, but they're not the same thing.

Self-Compassion

Self-compassion is the moment-by-moment willingness to hold yourself and your feelings with gentleness, and without judgment. It's a decision you can make in each moment, a choice to respond

69

to yourself in a particular way. Treating yourself with compassion doesn't require you to *feel* any different – it just requires you to *do* something different.

And if you do find yourself judging yourself or being harsh with yourself, you can make a shift at soon as you notice that – again, without self-judgment. In other words, you don't need to judge yourself for judging yourself. And even if you do find yourself judging your own self-judgment, you can stop the loop right there and avoid judging yourself for judging yourself for judging yourself.., well, you get the idea!

For instance, if you had a dog, you could decide how you wanted to treat that dog moment by moment. Even if you grew up watching dogs get abused – and even if you had abused your dog in the past – you could still change that way of being. Instead of hitting the dog, you could start stroking her gently, saying kind things to her, and feeding her good food.

And if you slid back into old habits and hit the dog, as soon as you noticed yourself doing it, you could stop hitting her and go back to being gentle and loving with her.

Many women who would never dream of being harsh with a dog are harsh with themselves. If that's true for you, we'd suggest you commit right this minute – gently, of course – to shifting that pattern. It is absolutely within your power to do that, and it will make a huge difference in your life.

Self-Love

Self-love is something that needs to grow over time. It's a larger way of being, a loving orientation toward yourself and toward life. When you love yourself, you do your best to appreciate yourself exactly as you are. Then, from that place of self-appreciation, you make choices that are truly in your own best interest, rather than ignoring, denying or sacrificing yourself.

The good news is that the attitude of self-compassion – which you can choose to adopt in any moment – will help you build more self-love. The more compassionate you are toward yourself, the more the love will actually sneak up on you and take hold.

Think back to the dog analogy. If you had a dog you'd been used to mistreating, you might not initially feel love for that dog. But over time, as you treated the dog with compassion, your love for her would grow. And if you deliberately cultivated that love, you'd soon end up adoring the dog – even if she was a funny-looking mutt with some bad habits.

(In a sense, we're all funny-looking mutts with bad habits! And we're all completely lovable that way.)

Practice: *Treating Yourself With Compassion*

Treating yourself with compassion means treating yourself the way you might treat a very good friend. It doesn't mean you see yourself as perfect; after all, if you know a friend well, you probably see her imperfections and "work in progress" areas quite clearly, yet you hold them within your larger acceptance of who she is.

So if you catch yourself speaking harshly to yourself, you can ask yourself, "Would I speak this way to a beloved friend?" Then you can shift your internal tone. When you notice yourself feeling something, put a friendly hand on your own inner shoulder, the way you might do with a friend.

Michelle: *A few months ago, Ruth and I left the house together in separate cars because I had to drop my car off at the auto mechanic. She was going to meet me there and then take me home.*

I accidentally spaced out and got on the freeway going south instead of north, so it took me an extra 15 minutes to get to the mechanic. When I first realized what I'd done, I berated myself: "How could you have been so stupid?!" Then I caught myself and said internally, "It's okay. Everyone makes mistakes sometimes. It's not a big deal. You'll still get there, it'll just take a few minutes longer."

If a friend were sick, you'd encourage her to take care of herself. If she were hungry, you'd give her food. If she were tired, you'd tell her to rest. If she just needed to talk, you'd do your best to listen supportively. *You can do all the same things with yourself.*

You already know how to act with self-love and self-compassion, and you probably act that way with many people in your life – so cultivating those qualities just means extending that same kind of attitude toward yourself.

Self-compassion isn't just about doing the physical things required to take good care of yourself – things like eating right, getting enough rest, and so on. Those are important, but emotional acts of self-compassion – being present with your own feelings, for instance – are equally important.

If you've ever had a friend or relative whom you knew loved you, but who couldn't listen to you at all – perhaps a grandmother who fed you soup and insisted you wear your raincoat, yet could never really allow you to share your feelings – you know it probably didn't feel very good.

On the other hand, a friendship with someone who listened well but didn't give you food when you were hungry wouldn't feel that good, either! That's why you need to give yourself both.

How Self-Compassion & Self-Love Will Help

We work with many women who are always the "givers" in their relationships – and in the majority of those women, lack of self-love is the culprit. If you don't value yourself and don't love yourself, you are likely to give disproportionately in your relationships in order to try to "earn" the love you don't believe you deserve.

Lack of self-love harms relationships in other ways, too. If you are harshly critical of yourself, you're likely to react very strongly to even a hint of criticism from someone else – and you may perceive your partner as critical, even if she's not. (We'll talk more about this pattern when we get to Roadmap Week 5, which deals with communication.)

If you're overly hard on yourself, it may lead you to feel very needy around your partner. Or, you might try to overcompensate for your feelings of neediness by becoming distant. Either way, it's difficult to have healthy intimacy when your internal environment is self-critical.

Self-criticism often leads to being overly critical of your partner, too. We've found that about 75% of women who are highly critical of themselves are also critical of their partners. The other 25% just heap all the blame on themselves. Either way, it doesn't make for a happy relationship!

If you criticize your partner, you'll probably find yourself feeling cut-off and lonely. And if you criticize and blame yourself, you'll feel bad, too.

Also, if you don't love yourself, you will have a very hard time attracting and accepting love from someone who genuinely loves *you*. You're much more likely to draw – and feel comfortable with – women who are ambivalent about you, unavailable, or even abusive.

Michelle: *In my past, I chose women who weren't good for me, because deep down, I didn't really think I deserved love.*

The problem was, the part of me that thought I was wrong and bad and defective kept trying to mold myself to fit my partners' needs so they would love me. But another, healthier part of me actually knew there was nothing wrong with me, so that part of me started to resent all the molding and over-giving.

That created even more of a mess – since of course I had trained my partners to expect that I would give to them all the time! When I started trying to change the pattern, it didn't go over well.

I needed to increase my sense of self-love and self-worth in order to be able to find and create a healthy relationship.

Self-love means accepting yourself as the whole person you are – including your gifts and your challenges, your strengths and your "work in progress" areas. It means being able to give yourself compassion when things are rough. It means becoming able to look at yourself closely and honestly, and keep appreciating yourself even while you acknowledge your faults, and the skills you still need to develop.

Self-love does *not* mean being egotistical, selfish, self-centered, arrogant or narcissistic. In fact, we've found that people who are narcissistic or egotistical actually suffer from a *lack* of self-love. That's what underlies their behavior.

Self-love also doesn't mean thinking that you're right all the time, or that you don't make mistakes. In fact, the more you love yourself, the easier it becomes to admit to your mistakes – because your sense of self-worth doesn't have to depend on maintaining some illusion of perfection. When you love yourself, you know that you're still worthy and lovable even though you're not perfect – or, as the saying goes, *You're perfect in your imperfections.*

The Brain's Ability to Shift

You may be thinking, "Sure, it would be great to love myself – but I just don't."

We understand. Being self-critical, judging yourself harshly, or just not accepting and appreciating yourself can feel so automatic that it's hard to imagine these patterns ever shifting. Lack of self-love can feel hard-wired and unchangeable. *But it's not.*

The truth is, patterns of self-rejection and self-criticism – or self-love and self-acceptance – get coded into our brains just like everything else we do or think on a regular basis. And in the past twenty years, brain science has repeatedly demonstrated that it is possible for human beings to *create new neural pathways* at any age or stage of life. Scientists call this phenomenon *neuroplasticity.*

In other words, it has now been proven that our brains are stretchy and flexible like plastic, rather than rigid like glass. This means that as we learn new ways of thinking, feeling and acting in love and relationships, the structure in our brains actually change. Over time, the new structures make it so that those new ways of being are easier and easier for us – until eventually they actually become just as automatic as our former patterns.

This process doesn't happen just by wishing it were so. It does take some repeated effort in new directions. *But it's totally doable.*

Look at it this way: if you're used to walking on solid ground, you will feel pretty awkward and scared the first time you get on a bike. But over a few weeks, if you ride your bike every day, your brain and body will get used to this new kind of movement, and eventually, getting onto a bike and riding will feel completely natural to you.

The same is true with thinking accepting, compassionate, positive, loving thoughts toward and about yourself.

Even When Self-Love Isn't the Problem, It's Part of the Solution

Not all negative relationship patterns stem from lack of self-love. And not all women experience a lack of self-love, or are harshly self-critical. I (Ruth) am among those who don't. Yet even if your problematic relationship patterns don't originate from a lack of self-love, building *more* self-love and self-compassion will help you heal them.

Ruth: I grew up the oldest child of very young parents, so I got used to being a caretaker very early in life. My parents always praised and appreciated me, so I felt good about myself. But I also developed a belief that everyone else would always need me to take care of them. In fact, part of my sense of self-esteem came from feeling more capable than the other people around me.

Obviously this became a problem when I picked girlfriends. I tended to pick women who had always been givers themselves, but then I out-gave them. Since they were used to being the giver, it felt great to have someone else giving so much to them, so they let me do it.

Over and over again, I created uneven relationships in which I was stuck in my childhood pattern – even with girlfriends who were fully capable of giving to me!

For a long time I blamed my girlfriends for not giving me as much as I gave them. Finally, I realized that I was the one who was setting it up that way. (It helped when one of my girlfriends pointed out that when she came over to dinner, she always offered to do dishes, but I refused. She also offered to bring takeout, but I refused that too. And then I felt resentful that I was always cooking for her and doing all the clean-up.)

Although my over-giving didn't stem from a lack of self-love, I've still needed to have compassion for myself about having developed such a problematic pattern – and also give myself love as I work on changing it.

Cultivating Self-Compassion

Whether you need to transform a pattern of self-rejection and self-criticism into self-acceptance and self-love, or just want to boost your self-compassion in general, we've got a powerful practice called Metta that will work wonders for you. The important thing is to do it for a few minutes - ten or fifteen minutes are ideal – once or twice a day for at least a month, so the new patterns can really develop in your brain.

The more you do it, the easier it will get. In fact, once you've done it for a month, you may enjoy it so much you just want to keep doing it.

Michelle: I worked with the Metta practice every day for about a year, and it completely transformed my relationship to myself.

I used to be habitually self-critical, and feel like I didn't deserve love. Now I find myself automatically feeling compassion toward myself whenever any challenge occurs – and I deeply know that I deserve love, and am worthy of love. This is a huge *difference for me, and it plays a big part in my being able to show up for the depth, sweetness and intimacy Ruth and I share. If I didn't love myself, I wouldn't be able to stand receiving so much love. I'd run away from it. But because of my work with the Metta practice, I don't have to.*

The Metta practice is adapted from a Buddhist practice called Lovingkindness Prayer, but we've changed the words for the Conscious Girlfriend version. We have found Metta to be an extremely powerful tool for helping the women we work with develop more self-compassion and self-love. It's gentle yet strong, the way water is gentle yet strong. The tides in an ocean or the lapping waters in a lake don't attack the land – they just return to it again and again, and re-shape it in the process.

Similarly, Metta doesn't do battle with your self-criticism or self-hatred. Instead, like the water, it gradually, gently yet powerfully re-shapes your thoughts and feelings about yourself.

If you can work it into your schedule, it's great to do Metta first thing in the morning is great so the effects can stay with you all day. Bedtime is great too, as long as you have the energy for it and don't fall asleep.

How to Do the Metta Self-Compassion Practice

Say these phrases, either aloud or to yourself:

May I be happy.

May I know my true worth.

May I know that I am lovable.

May I love myself with ease.

As you say these words, notice how it feels to say them. You might feel some resistance, or even a lot of resistance. It might seem dumb or boring. It might even make you queasy, or make you feel like you're pushing up against something inside. Any of these reactions are okay. Don't worry about them, and try not to judge them. Just keep going.

On the other hand, some people *love* this practice from the very beginning.

Ruth: *I'm one of those people. For me, Metta feels soothing, calming and wonderful, like spooning pudding into my whole being.*

So if you're lucky enough to have Metta feel good to you from the beginning, just notice that too – and keep going with it.

Even if Metta doesn't feel good at first, it will get easier with time. As you continue working with it, you may notice it sinking in, relaxing you, and even becoming something you look forward to.

Some of our clients have suggested saying Metta to yourself in the mirror. We think this is a really cool idea. But Metta works no matter where you say it to yourself.

Self-Compassion Practice, Stage Two

Once you've worked with Metta for at least a week, you can move on to working more directly with your negative or critical self-talk (if you notice it's still there.) Many women engage in a lot of this – sometimes without even realizing it. For instance, our coaching client Zoe believed she was very self-compassionate. But when we asked her how she showed that inside herself, she responded, "Well, if a difficult feeling comes up, I just tell myself, 'That's silly, that's ridiculous.'"

Although Zoe believed this was a compassionate response to her feelings, it actually wasn't. To help her understand that, all we had to do was ask her, "How would it feel to you if a partner said to you, 'Your feelings are silly and ridiculous?' Would that feel compassionate to you? Is that what you would want?"

Thinking about what she would want from a partner – and in fact, what she herself would give to a good friend who was having a hard time – helped Zoe recognize she hadn't actually been giving herself compassion at all. Yet after mulling it over, she asked, "So, would self-compassion mean that I felt sorry for myself, and pitied myself? Or would it mean I went to bat for myself in difficult situations?"

We reassured Zoe that self-compassion is definitely not the same as self-pity. And while it *might* lead you to "go to bat for yourself" if you were being mistreated or abused, it often doesn't require any external action at all. Frequently, self-compassion gets expressed by simply being attentive and non-judgmentally present with whatever you feel.

There are some painful circumstances in our lives that we have the power to change, and others we can't change, or may not be able to change right away. For instance, if you have an unkind or abusive friend in your life, you can simply stop seeing him or her.

However, if the abusive person is your boss, it may not be feasible for you to quit your job.

Yet even when the painful circumstance can't change on the outside, it's always possible to develop a different response on the inside. And when you do, it also changes the way the outer circumstance feels.

Many women who had painful childhoods (and even some who didn't) have a strong habit of self-criticism. This pattern negatively impacts both our relationship choices, and how our relationships actually turn out. That's why we've found it's so important to help our clients stop speaking negatively to themselves, and learn to replace self-judgment with self-compassion.

Here's an exercise that will help you do that.

Exercise: *Combining Self-Talk Observation and Metta*

As you go through the day, notice your self-talk. Every time you internally "hear" yourself saying something to or about yourself, write it down. You can also write down the trigger for the self-talk, if you choose, by adding "when…"

For instance:

1. I said "I'm so stupid" when I left the butter on the stovetop, and it melted.

2. I told myself, "Who are you kidding? Don't bother getting your hopes up" when I was opening up my email hoping for a message from Sally.

3. I thought "Boy, I look like shit" when I saw myself in the mirror after getting dressed.

After each sentence you write, say a *Metta* blessing for yourself. You can use either "I" or "you" whichever resonates better with you. In other words, you can tell yourself "May you be happy, may you know your true worth, may you know that you are lovable. May you love yourself with ease," or you can bless yourself, "May I be happy, may I know my true worth, may I know that I am lovable, may I love myself with ease."

As you work with this practice and the others in this chapter, keep the miracle of neuroplasticity in mind. Remember, brain scientists have proven that you can actually shift the physical structures of your brain by making new choices and thinking new thoughts. No matter how entrenched your self-criticism and self-judgment are, you *can* change them into a habit of self-love and self-compassion instead.

There are many other self-compassion and self-love practices we teach our clients and students, but this is a good place to start. We believe you'll find that just by using these simple tools, you'll reap great rewards – both in your relationship with yourself, and in your relationship possibilities with others, including the partner you seek.

CHAPTER 6

Roadmap Week 3: Complete Your Unfinished Business

✓ Come to terms with what really happened between you and your ex-partner(s) – and how you co-created it. Then, *forgive yourself.*

Landmark: *Once you've completed this week's step, you'll be at peace with the past, and ready to create a transformed future.*

Making Peace with the Past

Why do you need to look back at your past relationships in order to prepare for the love you really want? Because if you don't make peace with the past, you're either doomed to repeat it – or else likely to create other unhappy possibilities (or keep yourself from dating at all) in an effort to *avoid* repeating it.

We know the thought of taking a close look at your past relationships can feel scary. As we've already discussed, lesbian breakups can be among the most painful experiences on the planet. Two women can bond so quickly and intensely that it may feel like your life is ending – or like you *want* it to end – when you are no longer able to be with the woman you love.

We understand. We've both been there too.

Yet when you look back at your past with enough self-love and self-compassion, it gets easier. And when you look at the past with a sincere intention to recognize your part in co-creating it, and empower yourself to learn how to do it differently in the future, this exploration can become profoundly healing.

The Past Isn't Dead. It Isn't Even Really Past.

William Faulkner said that – and I believe what he meant was that as long as the past remains alive in our emotions, it controls our present and our future. So, since the past is still with us anyway, we need to make peace with it!

"Time heals all wounds," people sometimes say – but we actually haven't found that to be the case. We've worked with many women who are still in intense pain, only a bit scabbed-over, many years after a breakup.

Understandably, this makes many women feel leery of ever opening themselves to love again. Who'd want to experience that kind of pain more than once?

On the flip side, some women plunge into a new relationship as quickly as possible, hoping to salve the pain of loss with the joy of new love. Unfortunately, if you've ever done that – either yourself, or by getting involved with someone else who was on the rebound – you've likely found out that it doesn't usually work too well.

Ruth: *I got into new relationships this way twice, and both times, it was a big mistake. The first time, after years of caring for an ill partner, I was so hungry for love, sex and joy that I didn't give myself time to grieve the end of a 7-year relationship – so I chose my new partner Lou very unwisely, based purely on limerence and lust, though at the time I thought it was love.*

You'll hear more about my relationship with Lou, and all the mistakes I made with her, later in this book.

The second time, three years later, I had just gone through the worst breakup of my life – my breakup with Sarah, which stretched over eight months because she kept pushing me away and then pulling me back toward her again. I knew I was still in love with Sarah when I met Leanne, but I felt desperate for someone to take my mind off the pain.

Of course, that was terribly unfair to Leanne. And although I didn't understand this at the time, I also couldn't attract someone who was truly available when I myself was so unavailable. My relationship with Leanne turned out to be a year-long exercise in frustration and pain.

So if the pain of a breakup can last for years or decades, even for the rest of your life, and getting into a new relationship before you're done with the old one is such a bad idea, what *is* the solution?

The answer lies in truly coming to terms with the past – understanding what happened and *how you co-created it* – and then fully letting go. Once you do that, you're in a position to choose a new relationship with discernment, and only when you're truly ready (but you'll be ready much more quickly once you've done the work in this Roadmap.)

Looking at All of What Happened

It's possible that your ex-partner truly wronged you. Maybe she lied, cheated, abused you emotionally or even physically, or did other harmful things.

It's also possible that *you* did any or all of the above to her, too.

And, it's possible that neither of you actively harmed the other – and that you both tried hard and did your best – but you just didn't have the skills or the compatibility to make things work.

Regardless of what happened, gaining more insight into the part you played in whatever happened, will help you move forward. Understanding is power. Feeling victimized by someone else is a very painful feeling, and it's even worse when you can't see what you did to create the situation, because then you feel totally powerless.

In contrast, once you can clearly see the part you played – even if it simply involved choosing the wrong person, and/or staying too long – you can come to understand why you made the choices you did, and learn to make different choices in the future. That puts the power back in your hands.

Making peace with the past doesn't necessarily involve forgiving your ex. But it *does* involve gaining more understanding about the part *you* played in that process, and then forgiving *yourself*.

Grief has its own cycles and rhythms. Losing a partner you loved – and your hope of a future together – is painful no matter what. Gaining more understanding doesn't necessarily mean you'll stop grieving the loss. But it *does* mean your grief doesn't have to lead to bitterness, despair or cynicism.

Self-Compassion and Self-Love Come First

Before you even try to gain more understanding of what happened between you and your ex, and the part you played, we suggest you do the self-compassion and self-love work in the previous chapter. That will help you develop the strength to be able to look more deeply at how you co-created the relationship, *without judging yourself*.

Once you feel solid in your ability to treat yourself with compassion, we'd encourage you to do a retrospective of your last relationship. In other words, take a close look at what happened, starting the moment you met your former partner or first had contact with her, or even before that.

Often, women enter new relationships when we're still not fully over the old ones(s), and without knowing or communicating exactly what we want from the relationship. The problem with this is that if you don't clearly know where you're trying to go – and don't get agreement from someone else that that's where she's trying to go, too – it's very unlikely that you'll get there.

This isn't your fault, and it's not hers, either. It's not about "fault" at all, it's just about understanding how and why things happen as they do.

Imagine getting into a car with someone you were excited about spending time with, and saying, "Hmm, where should we go?" If neither of you voiced a destination, you might end up just driving around for awhile, and then running out of gas.

And this might be okay with both of you, if you were open to whatever adventure transpired. However, if you really wanted to go somewhere in particular, but you hadn't been clear with yourself or her about that desire, it might be deeply disappointing – even heartbreaking.

Ruth: *I think I assumed each time I got together with someone that of course we had the same long-term vision – after all, doesn't everyone hope for "forever?"*

But the answer to that question is No. Maybe most of us hold "'til death do us part" as an image in our hearts to be lived-out sometime, but that's very different from actively wanting it – and being willing to do the work to create it – right now.

I see now that all through my 20s, 30s and early 40s, even though a part of me did aspire to the romantic vision of lifelong love, I really wasn't ready. A big part of me was terrified at the thought of being tied down, having some of my life choices cut off. – Do I feel this way?

I think for a long time, my real priority was learning, growing, and having deep sexual and emotional experiences. There's nothing wrong with that – but I never articulated that priority to myself or to anyone else. I never said, "Let's get together and spend some months or years together, learn what we can, and then part when we're ready for something else."

So in some cases, I got together with women who were more ready for forever than I was, and ended up hurting them. In other cases, I got together with women who were totally not capable of forever, but because I thought I wanted it, I ended up feeling heartbroken.

I could have spared myself and my partners a lot of pain by being clearer about what I wanted and what I was ready for.

Did You Ignore Red Flags?

Both in our coaching and in our own experience, we've found that the vast majority of the time, there are "red flags" early in the dating process – signs of what will later become major problems.

Most of the time, when a relationship hasn't worked out, we can spot red flags that showed up very early on, that we chose to ignore. Looking closely at what those red flags were, and, even more importantly, why we didn't let ourselves pay attention to them, is a key part of understanding our role in whatever happened.

As we mentioned earlier, there are some common things women tend to say about why they ignored red flags:

Well, nobody's perfect.

Who am I to judge?

I just want to give her the benefit of the doubt.

She's the best one to come around in a long time. If I don't stay with her, there may never be anyone better.

I'm lonely.

I'm horny.

The chemistry between us is so strong.

The soul connection between us is so strong.

She has so many other good qualities…

She'll change, or it'll get better, once we get to know each other.

I can help her heal.

I understand. I've said most of those things myself, at one time or another. But now I'd like to share a story about one of the times when I ignored some big red flags, and what the consequences were.

Ruth: *When I had been dating Sarah for about a week, her ex-partner drove by her house, saw me sitting on the front porch, and made a big scene. Later Sarah explained to me that her ex had thought they were still together, even though Sarah had believed they had broken up.*

This should have been a sign to me that Sarah's communication wasn't very clear. It turned out that she and her ex-partner Joan had broken up the year before, when Sarah had an affair. But once Sarah's affair ended, Sarah and Joan had begun spending time together again, so Joan had assumed they were back together.

At least, that's what Sarah explained to me. Of course, I never got to hear Joan's side of the story, which might have been quite different!

Ten months later, Sarah broke up with me, then resumed seeing me while insisting that we weren't back together. And three months after that, she left me again (even though we "weren't really together," we'd been spending every weekend together) to reunite with Joan.

That big red flag I saw in the first week could have saved me an enormous amount of pain, if only I had let myself pay attention to it.

Terms with the Choices You Made

look back at your own past relationships, the part you played may be obvious to you – or it might take some work to uncover it. But you *can* uncover it, and doing so is a huge step toward empowering yourself to do things differently the next time around.

In some cases, your main contribution may simply have been choosing the wrong woman, and then staying too long. In other cases, you may have made a more active contribution to creating an unhealthy relationship. (Although with Sarah I *did* choose the wrong woman and *did* stay too long, I also made many of my own communication mistakes – and you'll hear more about them later in this book.)

For now, the most important thing to know is that the power is in your hands. You *can* learn to choose a partner wisely and then love her well, and once you do, that will lead to the healthy, happy relationship you want.

Now, answer the following Retrospective questions for yourself. We'd suggest doing a separate Retrospective for each one of your relationships, especially if you still hold any hurt, anger or confusion about how the relationship played out.

Relationship Retrospective: Part I

- How ready was I for a new relationship when we began to date? Was I fully available for new love, or was I carrying baggage (old hurt or anger) from a previous relationship?

- How clear was I about what I wanted from a relationship? Had I developed a detailed relationship vision? And if so, did I communicate that from the start?

- How ready was I to create and live out the vision I held?

- Were there any "red flags" when we first began dating – early signs of what later would become a big problem?

- If so, did I pay full attention to those red flags – or did I ignore them and just tell myself "It'll get better with time" or "It's not a big deal"?

- If I ignored the red flags, why did I do that?

Self-Compassion and Self-Forgiveness

Once you recognize the part you played, the next step is to forgive yourself. That takes having plenty of self-compassion. It also means recognizing that you were doing the best you could with the information and understandings you had at the time. Of course you know more now than you did then. Hindsight really is 20-20.

It also helps to remember that, like most people, you probably grew up without great models for healthy, happy dating and relationships. Plus, like all human beings (and all mammals, in general), you've got a deep hunger for love, connection, touch and sex.

These hungers are natural, normal and healthy. There's nothing wrong with our deep desire to love and be loved, or with our powerful sexual drives. But we *can* learn how to handle our hearts – and other peoples' hearts – with care.

Once you acknowledge the part you played in co-creating your past, you can choose to say, "I forgive myself for not knowing how to do this better in the past – and I intend to honor myself now by learning whatever I need to know to get different results in the future."

The Relationship Retrospective: Part II will help you focus your attention on some of what you need to learn in order to get those different results – because it's focused not only on your ability to assess the other women you date, but on your own skills.

Again, we'd suggest doing a separate Retrospective for each relationship about which you still have feelings.

Relationship Retrospective: Part II

- How able was I to *self-responsibly* communicate what I felt, wanted and needed?

- How able was my partner to hear me without defensiveness, blame, or trying to take care of me at her own expense?

- How able was my partner to *self-responsibly* communicate what she felt, wanted and needed?

- How able was I to hear her without getting defensive and blaming her, or trying to take care of her at my own expense?

- How able was I to handle my own emotional triggers when they came up, so they didn't have to lead to fights?

- How able was she to handle her own emotional triggers?

- Did I criticize her? Did I criticize myself?

- Did she criticize me? Did she criticize herself?

The answers to these questions will give you a lot of clues about some important areas of learning for you. As we said earlier, to create the relationship you really want, you not only need to find the right partner, you also need to *be* the right partner.

We've already provided some tools for shifting patterns of self-criticism, and in later weeks of the Roadmap, we'll go over the skills to listen and hear without defensive and blame, and dismantle your emotional triggers. We'll also talk more about how to assess the women you date to see whether they have those skills, too.

We hope the process of doing these Retrospectives has been illuminating and healing for you, but we know it may have brought up sadness, too. It can be painful to recognize the ways that we ourselves haven't fully shown up for the love we wanted, as well as the ways others disappointed us.

If sadness comes up, we urge you to treat it – and yourself – with tenderness and compassion, and say some extra Metta blessings. The next chapter, on Befriending Your Feelings, should help you, too.

We also want to remind you that understanding gives you power. Now that you can see more about what actually happened, and why, you're in a much better position to create a different relationship future for yourself.

CHAPTER 7

Roadmap Week 4:
Know & Befriend Your Own Emotions

If you're like most women, you really want to be understood by your partner. Yet if you don't understand yourself, it's much harder for anyone else to understand you.

In contrast, when you know what you feel when you feel it – and can accept your feelings, rather than ignoring or criticizing them – relationships work much better. When you become intimate with yourself, it's much easier for you to develop and sustain intimacy with others.

Befriending Your Emotions

According to our mentors Gay and Katie Hendricks, the five core emotions are sadness, fear, anger, joy and sexual feelings. All of our other feelings – like resentment, disappointment, worry, annoyance and anxiety – are just variations on the theme.

Although we all have lots of emotions, most of us aren't terribly friendly toward them, at least not toward the emotions we see as "negative." Yet by trying to shove these emotions out of sight, we actually make them stronger, and increase the chance that we'll act them out in problematic ways. As someone once said, "What we resist, persists."

Think about it this way. If you were taking care of an infant and she started crying, what would be more likely to help her stop: picking her up and holding her, or shoving her into the closet?

Many of us try to shove our feelings into the closet so we won't have to hear them any more. When we do that, they only cry louder, just as a real infant would. "Befriending your emotions" means listening to them, and to yourself, with compassion. Here's a meditation to help you do that.

Meditation for Befriending Your Emotions

Let yourself get comfortable wherever you're sitting, and take a few slow, deep breaths in. Notice the support of your chair or couch underneath you, and allow your breath to nourish you and help you relax. Nice, slow breaths, long and deep.

Now, let yourself think back on something that happened recently, that brought up feelings in you. It might be a misunderstanding or argument with a friend, or family member, or co-worker. It might even be a brief interaction with a stranger, or even a feeling that came up when you read or saw or heard something online.

Now, place yourself back into that feeling for a minute, and try to really notice exactly what it feels like. Observe where and how you feel the feeling in your body. Is it a tightness in your shoulders? Does your heart start to beat faster? Is there an ache in your chest, or a knot in your stomach?

Whatever the physical sensation is, just let yourself stay with it and say "hello" to it. You can say, "Hi, tightness. I feel you. I know you're here." Or, "Hello, anger."

As you observe your feelings, you might find yourself getting caught up in the story of whatever happened, thinking things like, "I can't believe she said that," or "That was really stupid of me." If you notice thoughts like that, just acknowledge them, and say hello to them, too, but then bring your focus back to your body and your sensations again. Stay with the process and just take a few minutes to really, fully feel your feelings.

In addition to the physical sensations, notice if you feel anger, sadness or fear. If the feeling has another label – like annoyance, anxiety, or resentment – that's okay too. Just let yourself say, "Hello, anger, I see you. Hello, anxiety, I know you're here."

After giving yourself a few minutes to greet, acknowledge and sit with your physical sensations and emotions, let yourself come back fully into the room.

How was that for you? For some women, it feels good to finally stop fighting the feeling, and just give it some room. For others, it feels scary. Some people just notice themselves getting distracted. If your mind starts jumping around rather than keeping the focus, there might be fear underneath that, too.

Whatever happens, try not to judge it, or yourself. The more often you let yourself actually feel your feelings, the easier it will become to do it.

The 10-Second Miracle

You may also notice something very interesting. Often within a short time of fully feeling a feeling, it actually shifts. Gay Hendricks calls this "the 10-second miracle." His studies have shown that often, fully feeling something for just ten seconds is enough to help the feeling release, or change into a feeling of lightness, freedom and relief.

The key to this "miracle" is *not getting caught up in the story.* Our minds usually invent stories about why things happened. Once we get caught up in the story, we can replay it for hours, days or even years, without any shift at all. That's why it's so important to focus on the *physical sensation of the feeling,* rather than your thoughts about what happened.

Ruth: *I remember the night when I was waiting for my girlfriend Jana to come over, and she kept calling to say she'd be late – and then later still. She was supposed to be at my place at 6:00, and she didn't end up arriving till 9:00.*

I only got to see Jana once a week (you'll hear more about that later in this book.), so our time was particularly precious – and on this day she had chosen to help some friends paint their house, rather than being with me. The story in my head was that she was wronging me. She was inconsiderate, uncaring, and not making me a big enough priority in her life.

Caught up in that story, I felt angry, self-righteous and bitter. As I waited for her, my heart grew colder and colder.

But I had learned about befriending my feelings, so I decided to try. I lay down on my couch, pulled a blanket over my head, and dove into the emotions that lay beneath the story. Pain. Grief. Fear.

I cried. I shook. I literally writhed on the couch, grateful that no one could see me. I kept my focus on allowing the feelings to move through me, separate from my story about how Jana was wronging me.

It took a lot longer than ten seconds. Perhaps it was more like five minutes. But after a while, the strength of the feelings receded. They were like an ocean wave that had crashed and broken, and then rolled back out to sea. I felt clear and calm. I got up, washed my face, and was actually in a pretty good mood by the time Jana arrived.

Now, having Jana get there at 9:00 rather than 6:00 wasn't okay with me. It was definitely something we needed to have a conversation about – and we did, on another day. But by befriending my feelings and allowing them to move through me, I empowered and healed myself, while also avoiding an ugly fight with Jana. I didn't need

Jana – or anyone else – to be different, in order for me to feel better. The power was back in my hands.

If You're Not Sure What You're Feeling

It's not necessary to know the name of a feeling in order to feel it fully. Sometimes it's easier to identify a physical sensation than it is to know what the feeling "is." So it's fine to just let yourself fully feel the lump in your throat, the ache around your breastbone, or the heavy feeling in your gut.

But it's also true that the location of the sensation can give you clues about what it is. Sensations in the neck and shoulders tend to be anger. Sensations in the chest and throat tend to be sadness. And sensations in the stomach tend to be fear. Of course, it's entirely possible to feel several of these feelings at once.

By letting yourself get curious about what's going on – again, in a friendly manner – you can also learn more about how particular emotions show up for you. Sometimes it's not in the form of sensations, but in words or phrases that run through your mind, or perhaps images or pictures.

Ruth: *For a long time, I didn't consciously know it when I felt angry, but I noticed that sometimes I would start to have an image of throwing things. When I was growing up, my father used to throw things when he was angry. Gradually I realized, "Oh, when I start picturing throwing things, it probably means I'm angry."*

Feelings About Your Feelings

You might also notice that you have *feelings about your feelings.* For instance, it's common to be frightened by your fear (or also by your anger or sadness.) You might also be sad about your sadness, or angry about your sadness, or some other combination.

No matter how many layers of feelings you have, it's possible to gently acknowledge each layer and let yourself feel them. For instance, you can greet the sadness – "Hello, sadness, I know you're there" – and also say, "Hello, other part of me that feels really sad about being so sad."

Emotions feel dangerous to many of us. Some women find that they quickly try to talk themselves out of what they're feeling, or else automatically attempt to distract themselves. If you notice this kind of pattern, just let yourself acknowledge it, too – and then begin to feel around to see what feeling is beneath the pattern. Somewhere inside, you may believe something like this: *If I really let myself feel this, it'll kill me.* Or, *If I let myself feel sad, I'll never feel anything else again.* Or even, *If I really let myself feel this, I might harm someone else.*

These feelings are real, but they are not the truth. In truth, you are bigger than your feelings. And the effort *not* to feel them creates many more problems than the process of fully feeling them.

Our fear of fully feeling our feelings is often left over from our infancy, when we didn't have the skills and resources we have now. To make matters worse, many of us were systematically taught by our parents or others that feeling our feelings, or showing our feelings, was dangerous. You may have been ridiculed, shamed, rejected or even punished for your feelings. So it's not surprising that there are many layers of emotions locked inside most of us.

But now you're an adult, and you get to make your own rules about your emotional life. Befriending your feelings and consciously giving them space will actually *free you from having to act them out.* If you're grounded in self-love and self-compassion, not only will feeling your feelings not kill you or lead you to harm someone else, it'll actually help you be closer to yourself and others.

We know that developing new habits around your feelings can be scary and uncomfortable at first. It takes courage to try on a new way of being – so we invite you to celebrate and appreciate yourself for having that courage.

As with any other skill, the more you let yourself feel your feelings, the easier it will be. Over time, as you befriend your feelings, you'll grow stronger, more flexible and resilient.

Owning Your Feelings

People often feel that other people or circumstances "made" them feel what they felt. Our language reflects that assumption: *That article made me sad. When you showed up late, it made me angry.*

But the truth is, your feelings are your own. No one and nothing can actually produce a feeling in you – all someone else can do is *trigger* your feeling. And no one can take your feeling away, either.

One of our workshop participants once gave us a great image for how people trigger our feelings. She said, "Picture a glass with some muddy water in it, where all the sediment has settled to the bottom. Your interactions with other people stir the glass up, so the sediment rises. But they didn't put the sediment there to begin with."

The great thing about owning your own feelings – rather than believing that someone else brought them about – is that once you know your emotions are yours, you restore your sense of power over your own experience.

Look at it this way. If other people actually caused your feelings, you'd be at the mercy of what the people around you chose to do. You'd be helpless, knowing that someone else could "make" you scared, or sad, or angry at any moment.

But once you realize that your emotions belong to you, and that you can choose to bring awareness to them, befriend them, and fully feel them – and help them shift in the process – then you're empowered. No one can *make* you feel anything. Someone else can trigger an emotion in you by "stirring your glass," but by befriending your feelings, you can make the water (emotional climate) inside you clear again.

Michelle: *Last year I had a Facebook fight with an old friend. She misunderstood something I'd said on Facebook, and unfriended me. Although we hadn't been close in years, I felt really sad about it.*

So I spent some time feeling the ache inside my chest, and connecting with the little kid inside me who felt hurt and misunderstood, and also afraid she'd done something wrong. I told her that it was okay, she hadn't done anything wrong – and that even if she did do something wrong, I would still love her.

I wished I could change my friend's perception of what I had said, but I realized that wasn't within my power. What was *within my power was to spend time with my own emotions. After a while, the sharp sense of sadness went away. I still wished my friend hadn't misunderstood me, but at the same time, I also accepted that she had, and felt at peace with what had happened.*

Once you know how to befriend your feelings, the next step is to learn to talk about them in productive ways. We'll cover that in the next chapter.

CHAPTER 8

Roadmap Week 5:
Speak & Listen To Build Intimacy

Communication Trumps All

The bad news is: *Love is not enough.* No matter how much two people love each other, if you don't know how to communicate well – that is, how to speak and listen to each other clearly and compassionately – your relationship will be a disaster.

But the good news is, when you learn and practice the principles of what we call Clean Speech and Clean Listening, you can avoid many conflicts, misunderstandings and fights. (And when you add in the SCORE Process, which we'll be teaching you in the next chapter, you can heal the roots of those conflicts! But we're getting ahead of ourselves.)

Psychologists who study couples have found that it takes five positive interactions to counteract the emotional impact of one negative interaction. When couples don't maintain that 5:1 ratio, their relationship suffers and eventually ends. This means it's even more important to avoid negative communications – i.e. fights – than it is to cultivate positive ones. But ignoring, denying or stuffing your feelings won't work, because that creates negative interactions within *you* – which will not only be painful, but will also negatively impact your relationship.

So the solution is to learn to communicate feelings clearly and cleanly, in the ways that make them most likely to be heard – and least likely to precipitate a fight.

Clean Speech & Clean Listening

Speaking cleanly means speaking without direct or indirect blame or criticism. Listening cleanly means listening without *hearing* blame or criticism. Obviously, these two skills go hand in hand – and they're both equally important.

When you become able to speak without criticizing or blaming, the person you're speaking to is much more likely to hear you accurately. And when you become able to listen without hearing blame, attack or criticism, then you can respond in a way that lets the other person feel heard, and makes her more able to hear you, too.

If both people listen and speak cleanly, the conversation will be smooth and productive. But even if only one of you listens and speaks cleanly, you'll avoid fights – since as we all know, it does take two to tango.

Why Avoid Blame and Criticism?

If you've ever been in a relationship in which you felt blamed and criticized, you know first-hand just how bad it feels. Studies of couples show that criticism is actually the #1 predictor of divorce. The more criticism there is – or the more one or both people *feel* criticized – the more likely it is that the relationship will end.

The reason why criticism is so damaging is because we all yearn to feel accepted, understood and loved, and feeling criticized is the exact opposite of those good feelings.

The challenge is that it can be easy to blame or criticize someone without even realizing that you're doing it. This is "dirty speech." It can also be easy to hear criticism in what someone else says to you, even if she doesn't intend it that way. This is "dirty listening."

Many of the couples we work with are caught up in dirty speech and dirty listening, with disastrous results. Here's an example involving a couple we'll call Susan and Joy.

Susan and Joy's Dirty Speech & Dirty Listening

Susan and Joy had two dogs who stayed outside while they were at work, but they had agreed that whoever got home first would let the dogs into the house. Often Susan got home first, but she would get caught up in doing things inside the house and forget to let the dogs in. Joy got more and more irritated every time she got home and saw Susan's car there, and saw the dogs were still outside. For a long time she didn't say anything. She just held it in. Finally one day she exploded, "How come you never remember to let the dogs in?"

Sensing how tense and angry Joy was, Susan immediately got defensive. She said, "Well, you forgot to pick up the dry cleaning last week. I didn't have any clean blouses to wear on Monday."

This made Joy get even angrier. "Well, that's strange since you have a whole closet full of clothes you never even wear. And besides, I work longer hours than you anyway, so why didn't YOU pick up the dry cleaning?"

As you can imagine, Susan and Joy went back and forth in this way for hours, and by the time they came to their next coaching session they were totally miserable.

So, how could Susan and Joy have handled this communication differently, without blaming or criticizing each other?

Susan and Joy's Clean Speech & Clean Listening

If Joy were using Clean Speech, she could have started with a question rather than an attack – for instance, "Hey honey, I noticed the dogs are still out. What's up?"

And if Susan was also practicing Clean Listening, so she just heard Joy's question, rather than hearing it as criticism or blame, she might have answered:

"Oh yeah, I'm sorry, I just got caught up in straightening the house and forgot."

Then Joy might say, "Oh, okay. It'd be great if you could remember next time." Or, still speaking cleanly, she could make a request, like "I'd really appreciate it if you could remember to let the dogs in when you get home."

And if Susan were good at Clean Listening, so she could hear Joy's statement or request without feeling attacked or blamed, she might respond, "Yeah, I know. I'll try to remember."

Now, Clean Speech and Clean Listening sound simple, but in real life, they're often not easy. This is partly because most of us have a lifetime of habit of using unclean speech and unclean listening, meaning using a lot of criticism and blame in our speech – and many of us we also have a habit of hearing criticism and blame in our partners' speech, whether it's there or not.

Your parents may have communicated with a lot of criticism and blame – with each other, and maybe with you too. If so, this history may have left you with a default pattern of criticizing and blaming others, feeling criticized and blamed *by* others, or both.

Because of this, even using Clean Speech doesn't guarantee that whoever you're speaking to will actually hear you cleanly. But it does make it a lot more likely.

Obviously, if both Susan and Joy were practicing clean speech and clean hearing, there would be no fight. But even if Joy were the only one working on Clean Speech and Clean Listening, it would still make a huge difference. Let's take a look.

Joy's Clean Speech, Susan's Dirty Listening

Joy: Hey, I notice the dogs are still out. What's up?

Susan: Yeah, I forgot to let them in, but you forget things all the time too, you know. You forgot to pick up the dry cleaning last week.

Joy: That's true, I did. Well, everybody forgets things sometimes.

Can you see how it would be hard for Susan to respond defensively to such a matter-of-fact statement – and how, by using both clean speech and clean listening, Joy would most likely prevent a fight?

Of course, this works both ways. Let's take a look at how the conversation might play out if Susan were practicing clean speech and clean listening, and Joy weren't.

Joy's Dirty Speech, Susan's Clean Listening

Joy: How come you can never remember to let the dogs in?.

Susan: Oh, I'm sorry, honey, I got caught up in straightening the house and I just forgot.

Joy: We agreed that whoever got home first would let them in.

Susan: You're right, we did. And I made a mistake.

Again, this kind of matter-of-fact, clean acknowledgement would probably prevent a fight. If Joy did continue on the warpath after this comment, it would probably be because she was actually upset about other things, and just using the dogs as an excuse.

Of course, this kind of thing happens all the time – because in the absence of clean speech and clean listening, many people build up a big backlog of hurt, anger and resentment. When this is the case, you need tools even more powerful than Clean Speech and Clean Listening to resolve the issue, and that's where the SCORE Process – which we'll cover in the next chapter – comes in.

We hope these examples help you see the power of clean speech and clean listening. We use this technique in our relationship every single day – in fact, we use it all day long, in every communication. And the greatest result is that there's no "scar tissue" between us – no old grudges, secrets, unresolved hurt or anger waiting to leap out and grab us, or creating tension and distance.

But What if She Really *Is* Criticizing Me?

In some cases criticism and blame are really obvious. If your partner says, "You stupid idiot, you did that wrong again," she is definitely criticizing you, and no amount of clean listening will change that.

But a lot of cases are more open to interpretation, For instance, if your partner says, "Why did you take my clothes out of the dryer?" it might be a perfectly clean question – or it might be a veiled criticism. And even if she doesn't mean it as a criticism, you might still *hear* it as a criticism.

Here are some other examples of statements people might hear as blaming or rejecting – and which might actually *be* blaming and rejecting, depending on the speaker's tone and intent. Or, they might be neutral statements of fact.

Did you remember to buy eggs?

You know we have to leave in ten minutes, right?

Did you bring the birthday card for Mary?

Thanks for cooking, but I'm not hungry right now.

I'm tired. I think I'll just go to bed early tonight.

You thought that was a good movie? Wow, I didn't like it at all.

You forgot to eat the leftovers in the fridge, and now they're moldy.

There was a typo in that email you sent.

Are you going to be there on time?

Take some time to imagine how it would feel if a partner said each of these things to you. Would you be able to err on the side of listening cleanly, and assume she meant exactly what she said and nothing more? Or would you be likely to hear any or all of these statements as blame, criticism or rejection?

Ruth: *I'm much more of a perfectionist than Michelle, so when we're working on Conscious Girlfriend materials, I almost always go over work Michelle has done and make changes and corrections. Sometimes I get nervous that she's going to feel criticized (especially when I actually say things like, "There was a typo in that email you sent.") I'm always relieved that she listens so cleanly.*

Of course, I also work on saying things as cleanly as I can, and try to give Michelle lots of appreciation for everything she does well. But her clean listening gives me room in case I don't say something perfectly. It's a good thing – otherwise working on Conscious Girlfriend could lead to a relationship disaster!

Can I Absolutely Know It's True?

Although we've given many examples of clean speech and listening, ultimately this isn't something you can do via a formula or script. Rather, clean speech and listening require an inner process of compassionately observing and checking yourself – both before each time you speak, and as you listen – to make sure you're speaking and listening clearly and cleanly.

Listening cleanly can be a particular challenge, because we all hear things through our own filters, or through what Buddhist teacher Thich Naht Hanh calls our "internal formations." For instance, if you've been shamed a lot in your life, you probably have internal formations that can lead you to feel shamed even in situations in which the other person's speech was clean. This happens in all kinds of situations – with intimate partners, friends, family members (of course) and even strangers.

It doesn't just happen in person; it can happen via text, email or Facebook. And it doesn't just happen one-on-one; it can also happen in groups. The more unclean our listening, the more we will end up feeling hurt by things other people say – even when they didn't really say what we think they said.

Spiritual teacher Byron Katie suggests that people ask themselves four questions to help us break through our stories and internal formations, and recognize that our perception of what happened may not actually be accurate. Here are the questions:

Four Questions from The Work of Byron Katie

1. Is it true? (Yes or no. If no, move to question 3.)

2. Can I absolutely know that it's true?

3. How do I react, and what happens, when I believe that thought?

4. Who would I be without the thought?

We often use these questions with our coaching clients, but we sometimes call on them in our in-person workshops, too. For instance, in one live class, a participant, Lori, told a story about a dating situation that had brought up some shame and pain for her. She'd made a sexual overture toward a woman, and had gotten turned down in a way that left her feeling embarrassed and rejected. Then another participant, Kathleen, shared a similar story and joked that in the future, she would make sure to masturbate before each date so she wouldn't be left high and dry (or high and wet.)

Lori got very upset. She stood up in the middle of class and told Kathleen, "That joke was totally inappropriate. You were making fun of my sexual desire."

Kathleen was shocked. "I'm so sorry you felt that way, Lori. I was really poking fun at myself, not you."

"I can't feel safe in this group any more unless you admit that your joke was inappropriate," Lori said angrily.

The whole room got tense, so we asked everyone present to do some deep breathing and send compassion both to themselves, and to Lori and Kathleen. We spent a few minutes just breathing together, and the atmosphere started to lighten up a little bit.

We told Lori that we could totally understand why the topic had made her feel vulnerable. She had felt rejected on the date, and then re-telling the story brought up that vulnerability and added more on top of it. We added, "There's nothing wrong or shameful at all about your sexual desire. It's a beautiful thing."

Then we invited her to consider Byron Katie's questions:

1. Is it true that Kathleen made fun of me? (*Yes*, said Lori.)

2. Can I absolutely know that she was making fun of me? (*I'm pretty sure she was, because she was joking about something that had really hurt me. But I guess I can't be absolutely positive.*)

3. How do I react when I believe that she was making fun of? (*I feel shocked, hurt and unsafe. I feel alienated from her and from the whole group, and even from lesbians in general. I feel hopeless about opening up to people because they'll always find a way to laugh at me, even when I thought it would be safe.*)

4. Who would I be without that belief? *(I'd be much happier. I could feel safe again. But it's not safe to let go of the belief because then I'd be even more vulnerable than I already am.)*

We suggested that Lori send even more compassion to the part of her that felt so hurt and unsafe, and asked the whole group to silently join in.

Then, with full compassion, we invited Lori to consider the possibility that she hadn't heard Kathleen cleanly. It took a few minutes, but she gradually became able to recognize that Kathleen really hadn't meant to shame her, and that she really *had* just been joking about herself.

It was an emotional few minutes for Lori, but it led to a big breakthrough – because she realized that many of her conflicts with partners had probably come about the same way. She had often felt the same kind of hurt in her relationships, and had always believed that her partners were actually making fun of her. Now she saw that in some cases, her own listening filters might have been the issue.

Because she had a long history of similar feelings, Lori needed to learn and practice the SCORE Process – which we'll cover in the next chapter – in order to get good at listening cleanly. Clean speech, clean listening, and SCORE all feed into one another, and once you've mastered all of them, your relationships with both yourself and others will dramatically improve.

Making Requests, Rather Than Complaints Or Demands

When someone whom you're dating or considering dating – or someone with whom you're actually in a relationship – does something that bothers you, what do you do?

If you're like most women, you either say nothing – or, when you can't stand it any more, you either complain about it, or make a demand for change.

The problem is, none of these approaches are likely to bring about the change you want. If you don't say anything, the other person is unlikely to know what you're feeling or what you want, so unless you just get lucky, she's very unlikely to make the change you're hoping for.

If you complain, she's likely to get defensive, angry, hurt, or shut down. And if you demand that she change, she may not want or feel able to do it – or she may do it, but grudgingly. (Most of us don't like to be ordered around, so making demands, or feeling demanded-upon, doesn't build intimacy.) Complaints and demands often cause fights, hurt feelings and alienation.

In contrast, when you make a request from a clean place, you're much more likely to be able to get what you want in an atmosphere of connection. Let's take a look at how these different approaches might play out, when you might actually want to make a request, and how you could do it constructively.

Ruth: *Years ago, I developed acute stomach problems. Over time, I realized I could no longer eat wheat. But at the time, Michelle loved to bake bread and eat pasta, so she continued to make and eat those foods.*

I found myself feeling really hurt. When I explored the issue more internally, I realized that if our roles were reversed, I would automatically have stopped making and eating the food Michelle couldn't eat, at least when we were together. I believed that was the "right" thing to do, and because Michelle hadn't done that, a part of me felt as if she didn't care about me.

Fortunately, using my own version of the Byron Katie questions, plus my knowledge of Michelle, I was quickly able to see that this wasn't the case. I knew Michelle cared about me. And when I thought about it further, I realized that I didn't actually want her to have to give up eating wheat. Just because I couldn't eat it any more, why should she have to miss out?

I decided to tell Michelle how I'd been feeling – not because I wanted her to change her behavior, but just because I wanted her to know me better. I think I said something like, "Hey, I've been realizing that it hurt my feelings when you kept on baking bread and eating pasta in front of me. It made me feel like you didn't care about me. But then I thought more about it and realized that of course you do care. So I don't need you to do anything different." (Except it didn't come out quite so smoothly, and there were some tears.)

Michelle listened to me lovingly, without getting defensive, and we had a good conversation. After that, I felt a lot better about it when she ate wheat, because I was glad she could still enjoy it, even though I couldn't.

Now, how might it have gone if I hadn't said anything, and hadn't looked more deeply at the issue? Chances are I would have just continued feeling hurt and uncared-for, and over time, that would have eroded our connection.

If I had decided to speak up, but hadn't gotten clear within myself before I spoke, I might have complained or made a demand. That might have come out something like this:

"I can't believe you're baking bread in front of me. That's so thoughtless of you."

"How can you be so selfish?"

"If you loved me, you'd stop baking bread and eating pasta."

"I need you to stop baking bread and eating pasta around me. It's just not fair."

If I'd said anything like that, Michelle would probably have gotten defensive, felt badly about herself, or both. Given her sweet, accommodating personality, I'm pretty sure she would have stopped baking bread and eating pasta around me, but we certainly wouldn't have had a conversation that led us to feel closer.

And if she had a different personality, she might have said, "I'm sorry you can't eat wheat any more, but that's not my problem, and I'm going to keep eating what I please!" That would *certainly* not have led to more closeness.

Now let's take a look at a different food-related situation in which I did actually choose to make a request.

Ruth: *Over time, Michelle and I have begun to prepare much of our food separately, since we often eat differently, and on different schedules. For the most part, this works well for both of us. But occasionally, when she makes something I like, I feel hurt if she doesn't make enough for me.*

One day I came home and she had baked a sweet potato for herself. The whole house was full of the delicious odor of baked sweet potato – but there wasn't any for me!

Fortunately, I didn't interpret this to mean that Michelle didn't love me. I knew she loved me. I also knew that if our roles were reversed, I would have baked a sweet potato for her without even asking.

But I realized that Michelle isn't me, and that she generally doesn't know what I want unless I do ask. So I said, "You know what? I would really appreciate it if you could bake a sweet potato for me, too, when you're baking one for yourself."

And she said, "Oh, okay. I'd be happy to."

And from then on, she did.

Again, what would have happened if I had said nothing and just tried to "make myself get over it?" Nothing good.

And what would have happened if I had complained, "I can't believe you didn't bake a sweet potato for me?"

Also nothing good.

But because I was able to speak cleanly and Michelle was able to listen cleanly, I made a simple request, she honored it, and neither of us had to feel badly or have a fight.

Now, sometimes the issues we need to bring up are much bigger than these examples – but the same principles still hold true. And actually, often the smallest issues can bring up huge feelings. We'll talk more about why that is, and what to do about it, in the next chapter.

Communication Deserves A Book Of Its Own

Of course, there is much more to say about effective communication than we've had room to cover here. When we teach workshops, or coach singles and couples, we get into many more nitty-gritty communication issues, like:

- How and when to say No – and how to stop feeling guilty about it.

- How to handle your feelings when someone says No to you.

- How to make sure you're making a request from a clean place.

- How to sort through your feelings to decide whether you can fully and cleanly honor your partner's request, and how to communicate your response.

- How to keep your communication and listening focus on your own skills, where you truly have power, rather than getting caught up in critiquing your partner's communication and listening skills.

- How to make sure she really heard what you intended to say.

- How to make sure *you* really heard what *she* intended to say.

But for now, just focusing on the skills we've discussed in this chapter will likely make a big difference in your ability *to communicate and be heard.*

CHAPTER 9

Roadmap Week 6:
Gain & Practice the Skills Involved
In Healing Conflict

Every chapter in this book is important, but in some ways, this one is most important of all. As we all know, differences between people are inevitable, and when we don't know how to work skillfully with those differences – and the feelings they bring up for us – then conflict is the likely result.

If you don't handle conflicts with skill, you end up in a horrible cycle of fighting, misunderstandings and pain. That has probably already happened to most of us. And if it has happened often in your relationships, it will probably keep you single and gun-shy – until you know how to heal your triggers, your "buttons that get pushed," by conflict.

The triggers are the key. Getting triggered is at the root of all of our most painful conflicts and fights – so once you know how to work effectively with your triggers, all of your relationships will become much easier. Here's why.

What Happens When We Get Triggered

Human beings evolved to "get triggered" in order to stay alive. Early human beings had to frequently run away from predators –

or stay and try to fight predators off – in order to survive. Therefore, when you perceive a threat, a part of your brain called the amygdala actually shuts down much of the rest of your brain function, in order to help you respond effectively.

If you're running away from a hungry bear, you don't need your higher cognitive functions. *You just need to be able to run.* And if you're staying to try to fight the bear off, *you just need to be able to fight.*

So that shut-down of most of your brain, which is called the *amygdala hijack,* is a good thing if you're facing something truly life-threatening. But it's not a good thing at all when you're just having a disagreement with your girlfriend – because once your amygdala has hijacked you, communication won't go well at all.

Of course, it makes sense that the effective response to mortal danger – either running away, or fighting with all your might – is *not* an effective response to an argument with a girlfriend. And this is why triggers get us into big trouble. Once you get triggered, you can't think clearly. You can't access your wise mind or your larger perspective. You can no longer really see or hear the person you're in conflict with. *You're essentially responding to her as if she were threatening your life.*

Now, if you're actually with a physically violent person who *is* threatening you, triggers – and the brain changes they initiate – may save your life. But if you and your girlfriend just need to reach an agreement about whether to go out or stay home, or who's going to do the dishes, your triggers won't help you at all.

Triggers Are Everywhere

We all know that it's impossible for any two people to want all the same things, in all the same ways and amounts, all the time. In fact, most of us not only experience conflict with other people, we even experience it with ourselves. For instance, one part of you may want to sit and watch TV, while another part wants to exercise, or thinks you should exercise.

In this chapter we'll focus on working with conflicts with other people – but the tools we'll be sharing can help you reach a more peaceful relationship with yourself, too.

We've all experienced the way small differences can sometimes spark huge fights. For instance: You might be hungry, while your girlfriend is full. She might prefer to eat outside on the deck where there's a nice breeze, while you'd rather stay in the kitchen where it's cozier. She might want to go out with friends, while you'd rather be at home. You might want to make a big Thanksgiving dinner, while she'd rather volunteer at a soup kitchen or just take a hike.

She might prefer to wash the dishes immediately after eating, while it makes you feel more relaxed to just get to them later. You might like to do laundry frequently, while she lets it pile up and only does it once a week. She might like to drive fast, while you always go the speed limit. You might like to have music on all the time, while she prefers silence.

And so on…

If you're not triggered, these probably look like minor differences – and from one standpoint, they are. Yet when we get triggered, even minor differences can lead to huge fights. Little things can come to feel bigger and bigger, as your amygdala gets hijacked, your body chemistry starts telling you you're in mortal danger, and most of your cognitive brain goes offline.

That's when your girlfriend's fast driving might feel to you like an expression of profound disrespect ("She doesn't care at all about my safety or well-being," says your amygdala.) Your leaving the dishes in the sink till later might make her feel the same way ("My wishes don't matter at all to her," her amygdala might say.) Pretty soon, everything starts to feel like a problem to both of you – because each person's triggers end up triggering the other person, so you're in a veritable cascade.

Ruth: *I've been there. I remember having huge, incredibly painful fights with my partner Leanne. It seemed like almost anything could set us off, and often it wasn't even clear what we were fighting "about." Everything just seemed to roll together into one huge, painful ball which eventually crushed all our good will and love.*

We're very excited to share the SCORE Process with you, because it's the most effective tool we've ever encountered for healing conflict at its root. It has changed our lives, and the lives of the women we work with – and we believe it will change yours, too, if you learn and apply it.

But before we tell you more about SCORE, let's explore some of the more common responses to conflict, the approaches that are already in our repertoires.

Fighting

We all know what it feels like to have a fight, even though we don't all fight in exactly the same ways. Some of us yell at each other, perhaps hurling insults or saying deliberately hurtful things. Others throw things, punch things, or even physically hurt each other. Some fight more softly, with lots of tears.

Whatever your fighting style may be, fighting not only feels bad, it *is* bad – both for our well-being and for our relationships. We emerge from fights weary and drained. It takes a lot of work to make up. And as we mentioned in the last chapter, studies show that it takes five positive interactions to counteract one negative one – so if you fight often, your relationship is definitely running in the emotional red.

Some couples turbo-charge their making-up process by having after-fight sex. But many others can't get close enough to make love for days, weeks, months or even years after a big fight. Frankly, we think this is one big cause of lesbian bed death.

Even after the immediate pain and wariness recede, *each fight erodes a little more of the love and trust.* No one can trust quite as much, or feel quite as safe, after a fight.

And of course, most couples don't fight just once. In fact, many have the same fights, over and over. Some couples fight more days than not, while others go a week or two without a fight, but then have a big one. Either way, fighting leads to brittleness between partners, rather than comfort and ease. Some people walk on egg-shells, trying to avoid the next skirmish. Other people just resign themselves to the inevitable, or even try to convince themselves that fighting is normal and healthy.

Most couples counselors try to help people learn to "fight fair." We disagree with this approach. In our opinion, no fight is a good fight, and fights are completely unnecessary – though it *is* important to have a way to handle conflict. The SCORE Process will give you that.

Storming Out

Instead of fighting, or in the middle of a fight, some women storm out – perhaps leaving and loudly slamming the door behind them. Although sometimes it's to "teach her partner a lesson," often the person who storms out doesn't really intend to; she just feels so emotionally overwhelmed that she doesn't know what else to do. She might even feel as if she needs to leave in order to prevent herself from saying hurtful things, or even becoming violent. In that case, her leaving may be a good thing, but if she can't communicate to her partner about what she's doing and why, it will still be damaging.

Shutting Down

Some women shut down instead of fighting or storming out. This might mean you stop talking to your partner for hours, days, or even weeks. This, too, is traumatic for both people. It's very painful to feel so unable to communicate – or so angry that you refuse to allow yourself to communicate. And it's very painful to be on the other end of this kind of silence, too. When a partner stops speaking to you, it's frightening, disorienting – and perhaps infuriating too. Like fighting, it erodes the sense of safety and connection.

Again, sometimes a woman actively tries to punish her partner with silence. But often she doesn't *intend* to inflict "the silent treatment;" she just doesn't know how to communicate what's going on inside of her. She might actually keep herself from talking because she's afraid of starting a fight – even though staying silent can do just as much damage in a different way.

A variation on this theme involves continuing to talk to your partner in general, but refusing to talk about whatever sparked your disagreement. This kind of shut-down can make the other person even more frantic.

Stuffing It

Conflict is so unpleasant and scary that some women just try to stuff their emotions underground. You might tell your partner, and even yourself, that you're fine, everything's fine, you've dealt with it, you've let go, it's not a big deal, and there's nothing to talk about.

But inside, the feelings are still there. You've just bound and gagged them.

"Stuffing it" can definitely smooth things over in the short term. In the long term, however, it's a disaster. After all, if you stuff your feelings inside yourself for years, you're bound to run out of room in there. Eventually, there's likely to be an explosion.

And stuffing your feelings also interferes with the free flow of other feelings – like love, tenderness and passion. We've found that this, too, can be a big cause of lesbian bed death.

But the damage of stuffing feelings goes beyond just cutting off sexual flow. The truth is, it's impossible to remain "in love" when you're consistently shoving parts of yourself out of sight. If you've ever heard a story about someone just leaving their relationship with no advance warning, it's likely to be because she just couldn't "stuff it" any longer.

Another consequence of stuffing your feelings is that they're likely to show up in your body, in the form of physical symptoms. Headaches, chronic fatigue, adrenal burnout and even heart disease are just a few of the many ailments that have been linked to unexpressed emotions. Obviously, stuffing feelings down is not a viable long-term strategy, and doesn't lead to happy, healthy relationships.

Processing

It's easy to rule out fighting, storming out, shutting down, and stuffing it as healthy conflict resolution strategies. But there is one last ineffective conflict resolution strategy that deserves a more in-depth discussion, because it's very common among lesbians. That strategy is Processing.

Our definition of "processing" is telling someone else what you feel – often at great length – *without taking full responsibility for your feelings*. The hallmark of processing is an undertone – perhaps somewhat disguised, but still present – of trying to convince the other person that she was wrong, and trying to get her to change.

Processing is seductive. It looks better than all the other alternatives, since it does involve communication. But if you've ever spent hours processing with your girlfriend, how did you feel afterward? Did the processing make you feel tender, close, reconnected, energized and optimistic? (If so, it wasn't what we're calling "processing" here.) On the other hand, if you felt bruised, exhausted, drained and wary, then you've experienced processing at its worst.

In our experience, the latter is much more common. The damage caused by processing isn't quite as immediately apparent as that caused by fighting. Fights are like explosions – they make a lot of noise, and everyone knows they've happened. The effects of processing are more like poison slowly dripping into a well. Over time, the water you draw from that well just doesn't taste good any more, even if you don't exactly know why.

The big problem with processing is that usually one person begins to process when she's triggered. That is, she's in the grip of strong emotions that were triggered by, though not actually *caused* by, an interaction with her partner. Since she's speaking from a triggered place, her partner gets triggered, too.

And two people who are triggered are in the worst possible place to have a productive conversation, or actually get to the root of their conflict. Even *one* person who is triggered can't get to the root of her conflict – and when two people who are both triggered are attempting to communicate, all hell will often break loose, as each person's amygdala responds to the other as a mortal threat.

The Triggers Are the Culprit

Once you get triggered, a chain reaction of brain processes gets set off which are impossible for you to think or talk yourself out of. These processes are designed to help keep you alive in the most physically threatening situations imaginable, which means they're very powerful. So you can't overpower them. You have to dismantle them instead.

The SCORE Process works because it helps you release the physiological effects of the trigger, and actually bring your cognitive brain back online. Only after you've done that can you get to the root of the conflict and heal it. And doing so requires many of the other skills we've already talked about, including self-compassion, the ability to befriend your feelings, and the ability to question what you think has happened, as the Byron Katie questions can help you do.

The SCORE Process – A Technique to Healing Conflict at Its Source

SCORE stands for:

S	**Step back into yourself**
C	**Connect to yourself with compassion**
O	**Open to and observe the origins of your feelings**
R	**Remember responsibility for your feelings** *(and relinquish responsibility for hers)*
E	**Experience empowerment.**

Let's go through those steps one by one.

S – Step back into yourself

When you're locked in a state of conflict with someone you love, part of the pain and fear come from feeling so *disconnected*. It may feel as if the only thing that could return you to well-being is connection with that other person – but at the same time, you might feel so angry or hurt that you don't even want to connect with them.

The great news is that you can give that emotional connection to yourself. And as you do this, you calm down the cascade of brain reactions caused by getting triggered.

What does it mean to "step back into yourself?" We might also think of this as reconnecting with yourself, your own center. When we're in conflict with someone else, we tend to be focused outside ourselves, on the other person. Simply reminding yourself to turn your focus back to yourself – not to your story about what's happening, but to your *physical* self – helps you get untriggered.

Until stepping back into yourself becomes automatic – which it will, after you've practiced SCORE for a while – it usually needs to start with a decision. You might need to say something like this to yourself: "Even though I'm upset with so-and-so right now, I'm going to consciously choose to pull back into myself. That means I'm going to stop thinking about what *she* did or didn't do, and bring all my emotional energy back to *me.*"

You might think your emotional energy was already focused on yourself, since you were caught up in feeling hurt or angry or wronged. But it's a whole different thing to connect with yourself in a manner separate from your feelings for or about someone else.

One good way to start is by paying attention to your physical breath. Consciously slow your breathing down, and deepen it. Then, as you draw a long breath in, let yourself pay close attention to the physical sensation of that breath coming in, and as you release it, pay equally close attention to the feeling of your out-breath.

Of course, physiologically speaking, your breath is a function of your autonomic nervous system. As such, it's part of the vast intelligence of your body. It works ceaselessly in the background, never requiring your conscious awareness to do its job.

But more metaphorically, I like to think of the breath as being like a wise, deeply present part of ourselves that can serve as a companion, teacher or guide. Even though it can function without our conscious attention, when we do turn our conscious attention toward it, we can work with it even more powerfully and effectively – and it can work with *us* more effectively, too.

So, paying attention to your own breath – the long, gentle in and out of it; the way it always knows exactly what to do, and finds its own rhythms; the way it never gets confused and breathes in carbon dioxide instead of oxygen; the way it always sticks with you, no matter what's happening inside of you or outside of you – can feel deeply comforting. Acknowledging the breath in this way can help you step more fully into yourself.

C – Connect to yourself with compassion

Once you've come back into yourself, you're in a position to direct compassion inward. To do this, simply put your hand on your own heart, or wherever in your body you feel the most sensation, and direct love and self-regard there. Keep taking the slow, long, deep breaths you began in the S step, and sense or imagine a flow of compassion going from yourself… to yourself.

You can also say a quick Metta Prayer for yourself:

May I be happy.

May I know my true worth.

May I know that I am lovable.

May I love and be loved with ease.

Another way to do this is to imagine that you hold a flashlight full of love-light in your hand. When you put your hand on your own body, you can sense yourself beaming love in.

Compassion doesn't mean feeling sorry for yourself. It doesn't mean telling yourself you're right, and the person you're in conflict with is wrong. It simply means attending to yourself with lovingkindness, the way you might offer a silent, loving presence to a good friend in pain.

Another way to think about self-compassion is that you can transmit it from the mature adult part of you to another, younger part, an earlier self who didn't have the inner and outer resources you now have. However difficult your current emotions or situation may be, it's certain that you have much more wisdom, and also more knowledge of how to navigate the world, than you did when you were, say, 3 or 5 or 8 years old. So, it can help to picture that younger child in our mind's eye, and imagine *this* self – your present-day, adult, resourced self – bringing compassion to *that* self.

Your breath can also serve as an example of compassion. After all, has your breath ever judged or criticized you? Of course not – even the idea of that seems absurd. You've learned that you can count on your breath to keep caring for you, no matter what you may have done.

Even if you have to struggle to breathe – for instance, if you have asthma – the breath is never withholding from you, or punishing you. That simply isn't in its nature. And so you can ask your breath – a part of you that has been active since the moment you emerged from your mother's womb, and will be with you until the moment you die – to help you learn to treat yourself with that same kind of steady care.

Once you're well-grounded in the S and C steps, you can move on to the next step, the O.

O – Open to observe the origins of your feeling

This step is a step of exploration and inquiry. Now is the time to get curious about your feelings, rather than imagining you already know all about them. Closely observing yourself and your feelings is an extremely powerful step. It can lead to much more self-knowledge, which is a prerequisite for many kinds of healing – and it can help you become able to let others know you more fully, too.

However, it's very important that this process of self-observation come *after* the step of directing compassion to yourself; otherwise, your self-observation might shade into self-judgment. In that case, you might find yourself thinking thoughts like these: "What's wrong with me? Why am I such a crybaby/ wimp/ loser/ reject?"

Stop. If you're criticizing yourself in any way, you're no longer in the SCORE Process. The point of the O step is to learn more about yourself in a completely self-loving, nonjudgmental way. So if you find yourself blaming or judging yourself, go back and re-do the S and C steps again. And take as long as you need to. Just those steps alone will go a long way toward shifting you out of your triggered state.

When you're ready to return to the O step – whether it's a few minutes later, or a few days later – the key is to approach your feelings with an attitude that Eugene Gendlin, the originator of a powerful self-inquiry technique called Focusing, refers to as *interested curiosity.*

As you cultivate this posture toward your feelings, you can ask yourself a gentle, curious "Why?" about your emotions, rather than an interrogating "Why." In your curiosity, you might explore questions like these:

- Have I ever felt this feeling before?
- What kinds of circumstances trigger this feeling for me?
- When did I first, or most intensely, feel this feeling?
- Does this feeling remind me of anything from my child-hood, or from other relationships?
- What is the biggest fear or belief underlying this feeling?
- Did I feel this feeling during my growing-up years? If so, what were the circumstances?
- Did I learn this feeling from either of my parents?

When you start asking yourself questions like this from a self-compassionate, self-connected place, you may become aware of things that surprise you.

Ruth: *I used to have a pattern of working very hard in arguments to convince my girlfriends that I was "right." I never liked to "lose" an argument. This pattern caused a lot of suffering in my relationships, because of course, my insistence on winning arguments meant that my partners had to "lose" them – so even when I "won," I didn't get the closeness I wanted.*

When I explored my feelings about the need to be "right," I was surprised to encounter a very young part of me that thought, "If I'm not always right, no one will love me." I also recognized that I had learned this pattern from my father.

Now, as you work with the O step, you may find yourself slipping back into thoughts about the person with whom you're in conflict. If you notice yourself thinking, "She was wrong to say that to me," or "I have a right to be angry," you're no longer in the SCORE process.

Again, if you notice this has happened, just bring yourself back into the process by going through the S and C steps again. Step back into yourself and connect with yourself with compassion – and take a while to savor this state of being fully in yourself, and compassionate toward yourself – before going back to observing and inquiring into your feelings.

Once you've observed your feelings fully and learned as much as you can about them, you're ready for the next step, the R.

R – Remember your responsibility for your feelings
(and relinquish responsibility for hers.)

Once you've stepped back into yourself, connected with yourself with compassion, and learned as much as you can by observing your feelings, you're ready *to take full responsibility* for those feelings.

Taking full responsibility for your feelings involves taking ownership of the feeling – recognizing that it belongs to you. You might say to yourself, "I recognize that this feeling I'm having is *my* feeling. It belongs to me, not to the person I'm in conflict with. Something she said or did might have triggered this feeling in me, but she didn't *cause* it. It came up in me before I even met her, and it will come up in me again, no matter what happens in this relationship. It's mine to deal with."

Just as observing yourself with compassion is completely different from judging yourself, taking responsibility for your feelings is very different from blaming or criticizing yourself for having them. Let's look more closely at the difference.

An inner monologue of self-blame might include thoughts like these: "I shouldn't feel this way. I'm too sensitive. I shouldn't be having this reaction. I'm screwed-up, flawed and defective. I'm probably not capable of having a good relationship."

Once again, if you notice any self-criticism or self-rejection, you're no longer in the SCORE Process. But don't criticize yourself for criticizing yourself, or judge yourself for your self-judgment. Instead, just return to the beginning of SCORE and spend ample time in the S and C steps again. Then you can either skip over the O, if you feel you did enough of it earlier, or re-engage with that step, too, before returning to R.

If you notice yourself feeling discouraged, depressed or pessimistic, that, too, is a sign that you've slipped out of SCORE. When you're truly in SCORE – that is, when you're truly *in* yourself with compassion, and observing your feelings from that place – then doing the R step will actually feel good.

People often resist taking self-responsibility because we assume that if we stop blaming other people for our feelings, we'll have to blame ourselves. The truth is, blame is equally damaging no matter where you direct it, and it's also equally misguided. Blaming yourself for your feelings is like blaming the sun for being hot. Feelings are natural; they pass through us the way the sun's heat passes through the sky. We can't stop them from coming, but we can learn to hold ourselves and our emotions with compassion, and also to recognize the true sources of our feelings.

Your feelings are part of you, but not the whole of you. They are necessary, valid, important and inevitable, but they are not permanent or even "true." They're more like weather – real, but mutable. A cloud can cover the sun one minute, and be gone the next. Feelings can be incredibly powerful one minute, and, when you work with them skillfully, they, too, can shift very quickly.

Realizing that you are larger than your emotions – you contain them, you can tolerate them, and you have choices about what you do with them – puts the power back into your hands. You're not at the mercy of your feelings, and you're also not at the mercy of anyone else's actions or inactions. You don't need anyone else to do something, or stop doing something, in order for you to feel better.

Now, in this part of the R step, the emphasis is on taking responsibility for your own feelings. But many women also need to do an additional part of the R step, which involves *relinquishing* responsibility for *other peoples' feelings.*

The formula is this: You are 100% responsible for your own feelings, and 0% responsible for anyone else's feelings. Just as no one else can "make" you sad or angry, you can't "make" someone else sad or angry, either.

Many women tend to take responsibility for other peoples' feelings. For instance, if your girlfriend is sad or upset, you may think that means you did something wrong. You might feel you need to apologize, or get stuck in trying to make her feel better.

There are several problems with this. One is that it's not your job. The other is that it's impossible. You can't change anyone else's feelings. Only they can do that.

Of course, people who don't know how to SCORE may not be aware of this. They may believe you're responsible for their feelings, just as you might believe it. In that case, you'll need to work even harder at part 2 of the R step.

We'd suggest that you remind yourself:

Your girlfriend's feelings – or anyone else's feelings – are part of her but not the whole of her. Just like yours, her emotions are valid, but they are not permanent or even "true."

Most importantly, you cannot control her feelings. You didn't cause them, and you can't change them. *They're not yours.* They don't belong to you. They belong to her.

It takes some practice to let go of taking responsibility for other peoples' feelings. But the more you can remind yourself that other peoples' feelings belong to them, the more solidly you can rest in your own experience, bring compassion to yourself, observe your emotions and take responsibility for them.

Often, another person's feelings may trigger feelings of your own. For instance, if your girlfriend says "You ruined our lunch by putting too much salt on those potatoes," you may feel anger, guilt, sadness, fear or shame. Rather than apologizing, getting defensive or trying to make it better – any of which would be *taking responsibility for her feelings* – you can do a quick SCORE Process inside yourself.

In other words, just notice that you've gotten triggered, and go through the S, C, O and R inside yourself again.

Once you've grounded yourself solidly in yourself, you're steeped in self-compassion, you've thoroughly observed your feelings and learned more about them, and you've taken full responsibility for them – and relinquished responsibility for anyone else's feelings – then you move automatically into the final step of the SCORE Process, the E.

E – Experience empowerment.

Once you've done all the other steps in SCORE, you're no longer in the brain state of being triggered. If you've done SCORE correctly, you should feel calm and clear. Your breathing and heart rates are normal. You're fully in your body, and connected to yourself. You're in touch with your own core, your inner wisdom.

And this means you're empowered to make conscious, constructive, healthy choices in your relationship conflicts.

It's up to you to determine what those choices are, but here are some guidelines.

- If you were triggered by a conversation, the chances are good that the other person is triggered too. This means it's wise to wait until another time before attempting further discussion.

- Once you've observed and taken responsibility for your own feelings, there might not even be a need for further discussion. For instance, if you're aware that your girlfriend's clean-speech question, "Did you take my clothes out of the dryer?" triggered fear, anger, guilt and shame for you, you may not even need to tell her about it, since it's yours to heal

- On the other hand, even if what you've identified is yours to heal, you might want to tell your partner about it – but at a different time, and in a way that makes clear you're simply telling her what you've learned about yourself, not asking her for any behavior change.

- If even after taking full responsibility for your feelings, you feel you also want to request some sort of behavior change from your partner, it's a good idea to sit with that idea for a few hours or more, to make sure you'll be able to make your request from a clean place.

Life Before and After SCORE

Ruth: *I tend to be someone who feels a lot of strong emotions – and when I couldn't SCORE, that made my relationships very difficult. Waves of sadness, anger, frustration and hurt would pass through me, and because the feelings seemed connected to things my girlfriend had done or hadn't done, I would immediately bring up whatever I was feeling. This led to long, painful conversations, processing sessions and fights.*

I was "sharing my feelings," but not in a way that helped my partners and me to grow closer. In fact, these emotional episodes had the opposite effect; my girlfriends came to experience me as volatile and unpredictable. Sometimes (I like to think it was most of the time – but you'd have to ask them.) I was sweet, empathetic, caring, understanding, and a good listener. But when I got triggered, I could take both of us on a relentless emotional roller coaster ride.

The SCORE Process has changed that completely. Now I've replaced hours of draining, unproductive "processing" with a quick, constructive process that I do internally. And when I realize, through SCORE, that I do want to bring something up with Michelle, I have the tools to do it in a constructive way, so that we actually get closer in the process.

Michelle: *Since I tend to blame myself when a conflict comes up, the first two steps, stepping back into myself and connecting to myself with compassion, are the most important SCORE steps for me.*

Because I blame myself for things, it's taken me a long, long time to become able to hold myself with compassion. I never had any resistance to the O step, observing the origin of my feelings, though it did take me some years of therapy to become able to recognize my own emotions.

I tend to take responsibility for my partners' feelings. So when I do the R step, my emphasis is on saying to myself, "Okay, this over here is mine, and this over here is not mine. This is hers." That's a big part of what leads me to the E step, empowerment, because when I'm busy taking on all of someone else's feelings, I'm definitely not empowered to make a clear or healthy choice. But once I remember what responsibility is hers, and what's mine, I can speak and act from a clear place.

SCORE is the single most important practice we teach, but reading about it is very different from actually using it in your life. And it won't transform your life until you do that.

We hope that this chapter will get you started on that process, but we also know that many people will need more hands-on help to really be able to master it, and especially to become able to use it with painful conflicts and triggers. If that's true for you, we hope you'll contact us for further support.

PART TWO:

Successful Dating –
Here's How to Find Her.

CHAPTER 10

Week 7:
Overcome Dating- and
Relationship-Related Fears & Blocks

✓ Learn powerful body-based techniques for transforming fear – and heal your fear of rejection, fear of hurting someone or being hurt, and other dating fears.

Landmark: *Once you've completed this week's step, you'll
feel ready to meet women and date with confidence and
an open heart.*

Fear is a big player in most peoples' inner landscapes. We might
feel afraid of getting rejected, getting hurt, getting criticized, feeling judged, feeling lonely, feeling smothered, or losing our freedom. We might also feel afraid of hurting other people.

All of these fears are common and normal. Yet if we don't work
consciously with these fears, they can cause big problems in our
dating and relationship lives.

• For instance, fear can keep you from dating at all – because
  you're either too nervous to ask someone else out, or too
  scared to say Yes if she asks *you* out.

- Fear can stop you from saying what you really think, feel or want when you're out on a date.

- Fear can keep you dating someone you're not that interested in, because you don't want to hurt her.

- Fear can lead you to break up with someone you *are* interested in, because it makes you feel too vulnerable.

- Fear can lead you to shy away from certain topics when you're out on a date, preventing the person you're with from really getting to know you – and also stopping you from fully getting to know her.

- Fear can lead you to mishear things your date says, or misinterpret actions she takes.

Here's a great example of fear leading to mishearing. In one of our workshops, we had participants work with women they didn't know, and role-play important dating conversations. The fascinating thing about role-playing is that even though it's not real life, it can bring up real-life feelings. So when Joan and Lucinda worked together, Joan practiced telling Lucinda something she actually wanted to tell a woman she'd been seeing.

Joan said, "You know, I've been wanting to talk to you about something. We agreed early on that we would just be 'friends with benefits,' but over time I've been finding myself developing more feelings for you. I don't know if you feel the same way, and it's fine with me if you don't. But I just wanted to bring it up in case you're feeling what I'm feeling."

After her little speech, Joan noticed that Lucinda had a "deer in headlights" look in her eyes. Then Lucinda said, "It's okay if you want us to stop seeing each other."

Joan was completely puzzled. "That's not what I want at all. Where did you get that idea?"

Lucinda said, "Well, you said you wanted to talk to me about something."

As they talked it through, both women realized that Lucinda had gotten so scared when Joan opened with, "You know, I've been wanting to talk to you…" that she actually *didn't correctly hear* the rest of what Joan said. At the end of the conversation, she really believed Joan had been saying that she didn't want to keep seeing her.

Although this is an extreme example, fear creates blind spots for all of us – and of course it causes just as many problems in an intimate relationship as it does in a dating situation.

The practices we've covered earlier in this book can help you a lot with fear. Saying Metta for yourself, befriending your feelings and doing the SCORE Process can do a lot to shift you out of fear, and restore you to a place of calm and openness.

But there's one more practice we'd like to teach you, which comes directly from the work of our mentors, Gay and Katie Hendricks. One of their specialties is *somatic work,* which means body-based practices.

Gay and Katie explain that fear can bring up four different internal postures or states. Each of us has a habitual response to fear, which is called our "fear signature." It may be one of these postures, or it may be a combination of two or more of them.

The Four Fear Signatures:

- **Fight.** If you have this fear signature, your main response to fear is to get defensive, or to attack (either internally or externally.)

- **Flight.** If you have this fear signature, your main response to fear is to flee – to try to get away (again, either internally or externally.)

- **Freeze.** If this is your fear signature, you go into "deer in headlights" mode. You feel frozen physically and emotionally, and may even have trouble processing what's being said – as Lucinda did in the exercise with Joan.

- **Faint.** If this is your fear signature, you internally crumple up and collapse in response to fear. You may literally get woozy, confused, or feel as if you've been punched.

Many people combine two or even more of these postures in their fear signature. For instance, you might first go into Fight mode, and then into Faint, Freeze or Flee. Or, you might first go into Flee, and then into Fight.

All of these responses are a result of a cascade of brain chemicals – again, the same brain chemistry we discussed in the SCORE chapter, which is designed to keep us safe from mortal danger. Because this is an automatic brain process, it doesn't work to try to talk or think yourself out of it. Cognitive processes won't be effective in shifting you out of a fear posture.

The good news is that there are simple physical movements you can make that *will* quickly shift you out of fear. Because these movements signal to the brain that you're safe, they actually reverse the physiological processes underway, and restore you to calm much more quickly. The Hendricks call these movements "Fear Melters."

Each fear posture has its own antidote or "melter."

The Four Fear Melters are:

Fight is remedied by **Ooze.**

When you're stuck in "fight" mode, imagine that your body is made of melting chocolate, and let yourself physically ooze. Try it – it feels good.

Flee is remedied by **Sumo Wrestler Pose.**

If you're in "flee" mode, try widening your stance, squatting down a bit and placing a hand on each thigh, the way a Sumo wrestler does. This will help you feel grounded and solid.

Freeze is remedied by **Wiggle.** Physically start wiggling everything you can – your legs, your arms, your head, your torso, your fingers. This will unfreeze you and help you feel fluid again.

Faint is remedied by **Love Scooping.** Widen your stance and squat down a little, as if you were going to do Sumo Wrestler Pose – but then, instead of placing your hands on your thighs, use your hands to scoop some imaginary handfuls of love out of the air in front of you, and bring them into your chest. You'll be surprised how restorative this is.

Fear is a normal and inevitable part of human experience – but we don't have to let it take over and dictate our actions. Just as we discussed in the SCORE chapter, you are bigger than your feelings. So when you notice yourself going into a state of fear, try the Fear Melter(s) that work best for your fear signature.

Of course, if you're with someone else when the fear comes up, you might want to excuse yourself and go to the bathroom, or somewhere private, to do your Fear Melter. On the other hand, if she's someone with whom you feel comfortable, you could also tell her what you're doing, and teach her to do Fear Melters, too. Everyone feels fear sometimes – and everyone could use some help with it.

As Michelle likes to point out, from a biological standpoint, fear is our friend, in the same sense that triggers are our friends. That is, fear, too, evolved to protect us from mortal danger. But in modern life, you're not likely to be running away from hungry tigers and bears, so if you don't work consciously with your fears, they may keep you from the life you want. The good news is that between Metta, befriending your feelings, SCORE and the Fear Melters, you don't have to let that happen.

CHAPTER 11

Week 8:
Learn the Truth (And Bust the Myths) About Attraction, Chemistry & Compatibility

✓ Understand what kinds of chemistry, attraction and compatibility are truly necessary.

Landmark: *Once you've completed this week's step, you'll know exactly what to look for – and what to avoid – in a potential partner.*

The Magic of Attraction and Chemistry

When you're attracted to someone, you know it. Your pulse quickens. You may feel a tingle. Your breath gets faster. You feel nervous and excited. You probably feel shy in her presence, yet you also crave being around her.

When you have chemistry with someone, even casually brushing your arm against her can feel almost like an electric shock. All of your sensations are magnified. Just talking to her on the phone, or feeling your hand on your shoulder, might make you sexually aroused.

Attraction and chemistry are not exactly the same, but they're closely related. We often have chemistry to people we're attracted to – and even if you're not initially attracted to someone, if you have sexual chemistry with her, you'll probably soon feel attracted too.

As we all know, these feelings are exciting, scary and thrilling. They make us feel more alive. They're a wonderful part of life in a physical body. *But* they have nothing whatsoever to do with love – and very little to do with long-term compatibility.

Like so much else we've discussed in this book, the feelings of attraction and chemistry we've described above are the products of brain chemistry. Human beings are animals, and we're sexually drawn to certain other animals for reasons beyond our conscious understanding or control. That's part of what's so thrilling about attraction: the way it just seems to *take over*. But it's also part of what can make it so dangerous to your dating and relationship life.

So how can you both enjoy the excitement of attraction and chemistry, and avoid letting it lead you astray? Ah – we're glad you asked.

Understanding What Attraction and Chemistry Are – And Aren't

We all know that some foods that taste great aren't actually all that good for us. If we listened to our taste buds, some of us might eat chocolate ice cream for breakfast, lunch and dinner. (And some of us might prefer vanilla or strawberry, or maybe Haagen Dazs Rum Raisin.) Yet that wouldn't actually lead to your *feeling* very good, or being very healthy.

So, most readers of this book have probably learned to incorporate other factors in your selection of foods. Yes, the experience of your taste buds is important, but the way the food will make you feel half an hour later – or two hours later – is important too. So is the way it will affect your weight and your overall health.

The same is true for attraction and chemistry. To have a happy, healthy relationship with someone, you do need to have some attraction and chemistry. But she doesn't need to be the equivalent of a chocolate ice-cream sundae on your attracto-meter – and it's actually better in many ways if she's not.

We suggest that women look for partners who are a 5, 6 or 7 on their personal 1-10 scale of attraction – rather than an 8, 9 or 10. Being attracted at the 5, 6 or 7 level is more than enough attraction to create a deeply fulfilling sexual relationship – and it will help create a more *balanced* relationship, with fewer triggers, than being with someone who scores an 8, 9 or 10 on your attraction scale.

Ruth: *The hardest relationship of my life was with a woman who was a "10" on my personal scale. I was so crazy about her that I overlooked all kinds of issues between us. Everything difficult between us triggered me more than it would have with someone else. Our relationship wasn't healthy or sustainable at all, and I think part of that was just because of the intensity of our attraction. It was too much for us to handle in a sane way.*

Attraction and Chemistry Aren't Just About Looks

Many people think they can tell right away whether they're attracted to someone or not – and can even tell from a photo. But the truth is, all you can tell from how someone looks is whether you find her *visually* attractive. It's fun to enjoy the way someone looks; most of us like "eye candy." But attraction isn't just based on visuals, and for some women, visuals aren't even all that important. You might also feel attracted – or not attracted – by:

- The sound of her voice.
- The way she uses words.
- The way she listens when you talk.

- The way she makes eye contact.
- The way she moves.
- The way she smells.
- The way her face lights up when she smiles.
- Some funny little gesture she has, or expression she makes.
- Her energy, and the way you feel in her presence.
- The books on her shelf, the objects on her kitchen table, the things she suggests doing on a date… and everything or anything else that gives you a sense of how she approaches life and who she is.

Attraction doesn't necessarily equal chemistry, and vice versa. You might feel initially attracted to someone, but then find nothing happening for you when she kisses you. Or, you might *not* feel initially attracted, but find the world moves under your feet when she touches you.

When you feel attraction, or chemistry, or both, it's good to remember that although it feels thrilling, it means nothing about whether you and she have long-term potential.

And if you *don't* initially feel attraction, chemistry, or both, it's good to remember that although it may feel disappointing, it *also* doesn't mean much about whether you and she have long-term potential. That's because attraction and even chemistry are mutable and changeable, not fixed.

Attraction – Or Lack of Attraction – Can Change

Most people have experienced the way that attraction can sometimes grow. Perhaps you've been friends with someone for a long time, but never thought of her "that way." Then suddenly you get into a deep conversation, or go away for a weekend together, and see her in a new light. You weren't attracted to her before – but now you are.

Some of our coaching clients have a pattern of being attracted to women who aren't good for them. Later in this book, you'll read more about Sandy, who found herself turned-on in the presence of women with whom she really didn't feel safe. We have found that this kind of pattern can actually be reversed through Metta and other self-compassion and self-love work! It's just a question of unlinking the links your brain may have made between, say, fear and sexual arousal. Over time, as you come to feel more at ease with the feeling of safety, you'll find that your attraction to women who are good for you will actually grow.

Attraction can also change in the other direction. Perhaps you meet someone to whom you're wildly attracted, but after spending some time with her, you realize you don't like or respect her much. She might still turn your head, but the thrill goes away.

Some women find themselves getting attracted quickly and strongly. But for others, attraction tends to happen over time rather than right away.

Often, without even really thinking about it, we tend to focus on physical features when we're looking for someone to date. We often hear women stay things like this:

"I want someone who's tall, because I'm tall."

"I really like blondes with green eyes."

"If I like her face in the online photo, I'll respond."

We all have our physical preferences, and that's normal and inevitable. However, the woman who matches your physical preference is not necessarily the woman with whom you can have a happy, healthy relationship.

We actually suggest that when first dating, women try not to pay much attention to feeling attracted – or not feeling attracted – on a physical level. Take your time to get to know the person in other ways. See what your connection is like. Find out whether you and she are compatible in terms of interests, lifestyle, values and relationship vision. Most often, if it turns out that you are, attraction will grow.

Attraction Is One Thing – Compatibility Is Another

We've found that many of the women we coach are actually looking for the wrong things in a prospective partner – or else not looking for the right things. So what *are* the right things to look for?

That's a big topic – and some of your answers will depend on who you are, and the specific relationship vision you hold. However, we do want to share some important understandings about compatibility.

There are three different levels of compatibility, and while all of them are important, Level 3 is the most important of all, for reasons we'll explain soon. Yet Level 3 compatibility is rarely on womens' radar – it's not something that most of us have even thought about.

Level 1 Compatibility has to do with common interests and shared lifestyle. For instance:

- Shared hobbies: You both like to hike and backpack, you both like to salsa dance or square dance.

- Schedules: You're both self-employed, you're both morning or night people.

- Diet: You're both vegetarians, you're both Paleo, you both eat organic, you both love sushi.

- Where to live: You both love urban life, or you both love living in the country.

- Lifestyle habits: You're both neat, or you're both messy.

- Personality: You're both introverts or extroverts. You have similar ideas of how to have a good time, whether it involves sitting at home with a book, or closing the clubs down.

- Age: You're of similar age or in a similar period of life.

- Culture: You're both African American, you're both Italian, you're both Jewish.

- Tastes: You both love romantic comedies, or acoustic folk-rock, or science fiction, or jazz.

- Politics: You're both left-wing activists, or middle-of-the-road Democrats, or active in anti-racism work.

- Interests: You're both fascinated by science and technology.

You get the idea...

Any of these Level 1 compatibilities can certainly help a relationship go more smoothly – and if you don't have any of them, things might be rough. For instance, if you're an urban dweller who loves to party, and she's a country mouse who likes to sit home with a book, you may have trouble spending time together in ways that suit both of you.

There's no question that if you're both African American, or both Italian, you may more easily understand certain things about each other without having to communicate about them. If you're both morning people, schedules will be easy to work out. And if you're both fascinated by science and technology, you'll undoubtedly have some great conversations.

However, in the long run, we've found that closely matching up on Level 1 is not the best predictor of long-term happiness, for several reasons.

One, if you're *too* closely-matched, the relationship may lack the "zing" that comes from exposing one another to new ways of being. You could tend to merge and lose yourselves, your individuality, more easily.

But more importantly, Level 1 compatibility is simply not enough – unless you also have Level 2 and, even more significantly, level 3.

Level 2 Compatibility involves the intangibles – things like your level of physical attraction and rapport. It's partly chemistry, partly that mysterious quality that makes us enjoy time with one person more than time with another. If you have Level 2 compatibility, you just like being around each other. You get each other's sense of humor. You enjoy looking at each other. Your conversation flows easily. For you, she's got that "je ne sais quoi" (French for "I don't know what it is.")

Level 2 compatibility is certainly important. You could line up perfectly with someone in terms of Level 1, yet simply not feel anything for her, and if that's the case, the relationship won't go anywhere.

But because Level 2 compatibility is related to attraction and chemistry, it can sometimes grow over time. And all the Level 2 compatibility in the world won't help you if you don't have Level 3 compatibility, too.

So what is this mysterious "Level 3 Compatibility?" Read on...

Level 3 Compatibility involves having a similar vision for a relationship – and the skills to make that vision a reality. It means sharing the same priorities in your relationship life. For instance:

1. **Wanting a relationship based on emotional intimacy, depth, and personal and/or spiritual growth.** *If this is a priority for you, you need to look for someone else who shares this value, and also has the skills to create and sustain this kind of relationship – for instance, the ability and willingness to practice clean speech and clean listening, be compassionate*

with herself and you, and use the SCORE Process when triggers come up.

2. **Wanting a relationship that's centered on sex.** *If you've got this priority, you need to look for someone else who shares it, and with whom you're sexually compatible. Otherwise, the relationship will be an exercise in frustration for both of you.*

3. **Wanting a relationship in which to co-create a certain kind of life.** *If you've got this priority, you need to look for someone who shares your vision. For instance, if having children is important to you, you need to look for someone who also wants children. If it's your dream to move to the country and starting an organic farm, you need to look for someone who wants that, too. If you're retired and want to travel the world, you need to find someone else who has the desire to do that.*

4. **Wanting an activity partner.** *If this is your priority, you need to look for someone who likes the same kinds of activities you do. If your dream is to do political activism with your partner, but you get together with an artist who has no interest in activism at all, it won't work well.*

In leading women through the 12-Week Roadmap, we find that many women have actually never thought about their specific relationship vision – or if they have thought about it, they're often quick to put it aside if they meet someone who doesn't share it. This is a mistake.

Relationships aren't just about love. They're also about compatibility. And true compatibility goes beyond the surface level of shared lifestyles, dietary preferences, musical tastes and interests – and beyond the level of rapport and attraction, too.

We sometimes hear women say, "I know exactly what I want: intimacy on the physical, emotional, intellectual and spiritual level." But by itself, this isn't actually saying very much. It's kind of like saying, "I'm hungry, and I know exactly what I want: delicious food." The challenge is that your idea of "delicious food" might be vegan spring rolls, while someone else's idea might involve a big hunk of grass-fed beef.

We'll talk more about creating your relationship vision in the next chapter, but for now, just know that having a shared relationship vision is a huge part of compatibility.

We can't tell you what your vision should involve. That part is up to you. As far as we're concerned, any vision is valid, as long as it involves consenting adults who want the same thing. The important thing is being clear on what your vision actually is.

Think about it this way: if you want a vehicle, it could be a perfectly valid choice to get a bicycle, a motorcycle, an SUV, a compact car, a station wagon, a luxury car, a convertible sports car... or something else. But if you go shopping for a vehicle without being clear on your priorities, you'll probably end up unhappy.

You could get the best bicycle in the world, but if your commute requires 50 miles of travel each way, it won't work out well. Or if you buy a sports car, but need to tote your four kids and a dog around, that won't work well, either. On the other hand, if your heart is set on a convertible BMW and you end up with an SUV, you'll also be unsatisfied.

So the key to Level 3 Compatibility is *knowing what kind of life you want to share* with a partner – and then finding someone else who genuinely wants the same things.

For most of the women we work with, the ability to create and maintain emotional intimacy is an important value. If that's true for you, you need to find someone who both shares that value, *and* has – or is committed to developing – the skills to co-create that kind of connection. Without that, all the other kinds of compatibility in the world won't make for a good relationship.

CHAPTER 12

Week 9:
Create Your Relationship Vision

✓ Design your ideal relationship, and get crystal-clear on what it offers and requires.

Landmark: *Once you've completed this week's step, you'll be clear on your must-haves and deal-breakers, so you can quickly recognize who's right and who's not – and stick to your vision.*

What Do You Want?

What do you want from an intimate relationship? What do you *really, really* want?

What makes you happiest? What works well for you? What are the conditions in which you thrive? What makes your soul sing?

In all of existence, there has never been someone exactly like you – with your exact history, your preferences, your unique quirks, and your particular blend of body, heart, mind and spirit.

And now that you've strengthened your self-love and self-compassion, and befriended your feelings, you're likely in a better position to celebrate yourself than ever before – and, out of that sense of celebration, to identify what you really want.

Of course, a healthy relationship will always be the co-creation of both people involved. You won't be its sole creator. But the clearer you are about what *you* want, the better able you'll be to choose a partner with whom you can happily and consciously co-create.

Many of us never really ask ourselves what we most want. It can feel vulnerable, scary, overwhelming or even painful just to start asking those questions. It might bring up thoughts like these:

"What if I just don't know what I want – what do I do then?"

"What's the point of figuring out what I want, if I'm not going to get it?"

"What if no one else wants what I want – so getting in touch with my true desires will mean I'll end up alone?"

"Do I really deserve to have what I want?"

If asking yourself what you really want feels difficult, do some Metta for yourself, and befriend those feelings of discomfort and fear. Then remind yourself that you *can* find out more about what you want, even if the process takes you some time. And you can also get what you want, as long as it's based on a realistic vision rather than a fantasy, and as long as you have the skills to carry it out.

Women often express the concern that there may be "no one out there" who wants what they want, and with whom they're compatible in other ways. But both our personal experience (we're both pretty unusual people ourselves, and we met via a Craigslist ad. You'll hear more about that later), and the experience of our clients suggests otherwise.

And do we even need to tell you that *Yes,* you do deserve it?

All this choice and freedom can feel overwhelming. Yet as you settle into the idea of your own creative power, you may also find yourself getting excited by it. We hope so.

The more you know about what you want, the more likely you are to get it. Of course, the reverse is also true: the *less* you know about what you want, the less likely you are to get it. And that's the way most of the women we talk to live out their relationship lives.

So, we want to encourage you to do something different – something courageous, bold and life-changing: *Inquire deeply into who you are, and then develop your own vision of the ideal relationship for* you.

Not your parents' version. Not your friends' version. Not the Hollywood version. Not the default version. But your very own vision.

Recently, a participant in one of our workshops had a light bulb moment. "I just realized I don't have to live with a partner." she said excitedly. "We could live next door, or in the same building, or down the street from each other. We don't have to live together just because 'that's what everyone does.'"

We all applauded.

Recognizing the Possibilities

Imagine that you had no food at all in your house – say, you've just moved in, or just returned from a long trip – so you have to start food-shopping from scratch. What do you want to get?

Okay, let's start with fruits and vegetables. Which ones do you want? Fresh, canned or frozen? Organic or conventional? Do you buy the pre-washed, pre-chopped, pre-bagged fresh kind to save time, or the whole vegetables because they're both fresher and cheaper? Do you care about their glycemic index? Does it matter to you whether they were grown locally? Do you want them to look cosmetically perfect, or do you care more about how they taste?

You'll face similar choices in every other aisle. At the end, whatever you put in your cart will probably be a unique reflection of your tastes, your values, your budget, your health priorities, your cooking facilities, how hungry you are, and whatever other factors you choose to consider.

Now, imagine that as you pushed your cart through the store, strangers randomly piled items into it. Would you be willing to pay for those items you hadn't chosen, take them home and eat them? Probably not. Most of us have pretty specific preferences about our food, and take for granted our right to choose it.

So we're suggesting you take a similar attitude toward choosing the features of the relationship you most want to create. Relationships involve myriad decisions – and if you don't make these decisions consciously, you'll make them unconsciously, based on what your parents did, what your friends do, what people do in movies, what you think the other person wants (whether or not that's actually what she wants.), and other factors that don't reflect who you really are, and what you really want.

Must-Haves and Deal-breakers

Because there are so many different issues to consider, you may find it's easiest to start with three and three: naming the three qualities your ideal relationship or partner *must have,* and three qualities that would be completely unacceptable to you.

Here are mine, which my relationship with Michelle meets in every way:

Ruth's Must-Haves:

1. Conscious approach to interaction and communication; emotionally self-responsible

2. A larger spiritual perspective

3. An emotional flavor of ease, generosity, harmony and sweetness

Ruth's Deal-Breakers:

1. Addictions

2. Fights, tension, drama

3. Someone who tries to constrict or control how I spend my time, money or other resources

Now, here's the list our client Kaylee, 32, initially came up with.

Kaylee's Must-Haves:

1. Wants children

2. Wants to live in the country

3. Wants to homeschool

Kaylee's Deal-Breakers:

1. Sexual or emotional infidelity

2. Eats unhealthy food

3. Financially irresponsible

4. Alcoholic or drug addict

5. Emotionally volatile – shouts or withdraws

You might notice that my "Must-Haves" list is more about substance than form – that is, I am focused on wanting specific emotional qualities in a partnership, rather than sharing a particular lifestyle. In contrast, Kaylee's focus is on creating a very specific kind of life with a partner, including co-parenting, home-schooling, and living in the country. Neither approach is better or worse; they're both perfectly valid. But they do reflect different perspectives on the role of partnership.

At first Kaylee had trouble coming up with deal-breakers at all, since she thought that any woman who shared her vision would be fine with her, as long as they liked and were attracted to each other. But as we talked more, she realized that there were actually many things that would be rule-outs for her, so she actually listed five, not three.

As we went over her list, we encouraged Kaylee to get even more specific about some of her "deal-breakers." For instance, we asked her, "What do you consider 'emotional infidelity?' Would you be okay with your partner having close same-sex friendships?"

"Of course." Kaylee said. "It's not like I'd want to police her." As she thought more about it, she realized that what really mattered to her was emotional honesty. "I wouldn't even mind it if my partner had a crush on someone, as long as she told me about it," she explained. "I just wouldn't want her sneaking around and trying to hide it from me, or getting secretive about how often they were texting each other."

"What does 'Eats unhealthy food' mean to you?" we asked. "Is it okay if she eats fast food now and then, as long as she eats healthy at home? Or do you want to be with someone who'd never take a bite of anything that wasn't organic?"

Kaylee laughed. "I don't expect perfection. I guess what really matters to me is that we'd have an agreement about where our shared food dollars are going, and set a healthy example for the kids. I wouldn't want cabinets full of sugary junk foods."

The deeper she delved, the more Kaylee realized there were actually many qualities that were important to her in a partner and a relationship, and many that would be unacceptable. So after starting with Must-Haves and Deal-Breakers, she happily moved on to the Creating Your Relationship Vision exercise we'll give you soon.

Our client Georgia, 65, had very different lists than Kaylee's, reflecting both her different stage of life, and her different values and priorities. Here are her initial lists:

<u>Georgia's Must-Haves</u>

1. Fully out of the closet

2. Physically affectionate and sensual, though not necessarily focused on having genital sex

3. Loves to travel, and has the means to do so

<u>Georgia's Deal-Breakers</u>

1. Religious

2. Republican

3. Excessively introverted

When we asked Georgia to give us a fuller explanation of many of her list items, it turned out that quite a few of them were based on problems she'd experienced in her previous relationships. For instance, she had once had a partner who was so closeted that she hadn't wanted to be seen in public with Georgia. On further thought, Georgia reflected, "Well, it's not as if my next partner would have to be 'out' to every single childhood friend and all her relatives. I just wouldn't want to be with someone who's ashamed of who we are. And I wouldn't want to be limited in the kinds of things we could do as a couple."

Some of Georgia's deal-breakers turned out to be similarly based on prior bad experiences. She realized when she thought about it more that she could be okay with someone religious, as long as her religion was open-minded and non-homophobic. "I can't really imagine an open-minded Republican, but I guess even a Republican could be okay with me if she were thoughtful and compassionate," she added.

Now we suggest you make your own list of Must-Haves and Deal-Breakers. Start by listing three and three – or more, if you'd like – in each category.

Your Initial Must-Haves

1.

2.

3.

Your Initial Deal-Breakers

1.

2.

3.

Once you've come up with a first draft of your Must-Haves and Deal-Breakers, let yourself get curious about what you've written. See which items you can clarify or expand upon. Also notice whether you can dive underneath anything you've listed to uncover something even more important to you. If so, revise your lists.

As Georgia did this exercise, she came up with some significant revisions. Here are her new lists:

Georgia's Revised Must-Haves

1. We live a free, open, proud lesbian life together. We're both happy and comfortable with ourselves and our sexuality.

2. We are physically affectionate and sensual, though not necessarily focused on having genital sex.

3. We both love to (and can afford to) travel, with a focus on eco-travel, but we also enjoy our time at home.

4. We are both open-minded, nonjudgmental and flexible in our approach to life, communication and each other.

Georgia's Revised Deal-Breakers

1. Emotional, spiritual or political rigidity. Overly demanding or "set in her ways," or trying to dictate how I should be.

2. Emotionally unhealthy in a way that would interfere with our having an active, fun social and travel life.

Coming up with these revisions helped Georgia realize what a core value she had around open-mindedness and flexibility. Then, a few weeks later, an interesting thing happened. She found an online profile which really appealed to her – except that in the last paragraph, the author mentioned that she was a transwoman.

A lifelong lesbian, Georgia would never have previously thought she would be open to dating a transwoman. But now that she'd clarified her priorities, she realized it would be inconsistent for her to rule out a potential match just because she hadn't been born in a female body. "After all," Georgia reflected, "If what I care about is someone being free, open, proud and comfortable with her sexuality, this person certainly qualifies." She contacted the profile's author, they arranged to meet, and found they really liked each other.

To us, this is a great example of the principle of co-creation. Each of us gets to identify certain things that are uniquely important for us – and then, invariably, we also get to be surprised by some of the specific forms or packages in which our priorities may show up.

Ruth: *When I met Michelle, she was in seminary, and I had a private practice as a psychospiritual healer. I wanted to be with someone with a strong spiritual perspective, but I was taken aback at first by the idea that she was studying to become a minister. I thought, "Could I really be a minister's wife?" My spiritual approach was so alternative and mystical, and the idea of ministry sounded so conventional to me. But when we talked, I realized that Michelle's underlying spiritual beliefs and values were much like mine. (As it turned out, she didn't become a minister after all. But I would have fully supported her if she had stayed on that path.)*

Creating a Clear, Specific & Detailed Relationship Vision

Now that we've gotten you warmed up, we're going to give you a long list of things we suggest you think about, journal about, envision and sketch out in your mind. And, long as it is, it's still just a starting point. There's no way we could possibly think of everything that might feel important to you – so we encourage you to add additional categories or items.

There are no right or wrong answers to any of these questions. Their purpose is to help you get clear about what matters to you, and, even more importantly, *why* it matters.

As with the Must-Haves and Deal-Breakers, when you look at some of the "whys," your answers may surprise you. You may learn some new things about yourself. You may even find some of your answers changing as you delve more deeply into this exploration.

One reason why that can happen is because sometimes a desire is really just a proxy for another desire. For instance, you might initially think you want to be with someone who makes the same amount of money you do, so the relationship will feel equal. But on further reflection, you might realize that there are ways to create equality even with someone who makes more or less money than you do.

You might think you need to be with someone who has done more emotional and spiritual work than you have, so she can "pull you up to her level" if you start to fall into old patterns. But as you think through it more, you might realize that if you find someone who is truly committed to conscious, self-responsible relationships, you might be able to pull *her* up at times – or the two of you might just mutually support each other.

Your Ideal Relationship: A Questionnaire

Spirituality & Values

- How important is it to you to have a conscious relationship? (i.e., a relationship in which both partners are strongly committed to gaining and practicing compassion for themselves and each other, skills for clean communication and conflict-healing, and ongoing personal growth)

- What is your spiritual and/or religious orientation, and how important is it to you? Does it matter to you that your partner be similarly spiritually oriented?

- Do you prefer that your partner be of the same race, ethnic background, and/or social class as you? If so, why? If not, why not?

- Do you prefer that your partner be close to your age? If so, why is that important to you? What are your concerns about being with someone significantly older or younger?

- How "out" are you, and how important is it that your partner be similarly "out"? Why is this important?

- Imagine that the two of you are having communication challenges. How would you handle this? Would you go to a relationship coach together? Attend workshops together? Go to a couples counselor together? Read self-help books together? Something else?

- Imagine that your house is burning down and each of you can only grab three things on your way out the door. Which three things would you grab? Which three things would you want your partner to grab? Why?

Verbal & Non-Verbal Communication Styles

- Imagine that you and your future partner are choosing where to go on vacation. She has one preference, and you have another. How do you work it out?

- Imagine that you've come home from a hard day at work, and want some support from your partner. What kind of support to do you most want? How do you communicate about this to your partner? How does she respond?

- Imagine that you and your partner have had a misunderstanding, and you've had some new insights about what happened. How do you bring this up with your partner? How do you envision reconnecting with her?

- Imagine that you're sick in bed with a cold. How would you most want your partner to take care of you? (Some women want their partners to wait on them; others prefer to be left alone. You might fall anywhere on that spectrum…)

- How do you show love in a partnership, and how do you most like your partner to show her love? (For example: giving gifts, giving back rubs, going out to dinner, doing small favors for your partner, being present and listening to her with compassion, spending time together in the same room while engaged in different activities, etc.)

- Is non-sexual physical affection important to you? What does that look like for you? What would be your ideal?

- How do you feel about public displays of affection?

Time Together & Time Apart

- What kinds of alone time do you like and need? How often?

- What are your favorite ways of spending time with a partner?

- When you're in a partnership, do you prefer to socialize 1:1 with separate friends, do most of your socializing together with other couples, or...?

- How introverted or extroverted are you, and how does this impact the kind of time you'd want to spend with a partner, and the activities you'd want to do together and separately?

Relationship Form

- What is your fondest vision for your next relationship? (For example, are you looking for a lifelong partnership? Open to whatever evolves? Seeking casual dating only? Something else?)

- Do you hope to get married? If so, why is that important to you?

- How do you like to share physical space with a partner? Do you prefer to live separately, live together, live next door, share a bedroom, live together with separate bedrooms or space, or...?

- Do you envision sharing finances, or keeping finances separate? What's important to you about this?

Lifestyle

- What is your career/work life like? In your ideal relationship, how would the two of you navigate between your work lives and your relationship life?

- Would you be comfortable with a partner who made significantly more or less money than you, or had significantly more or fewer assets? Why or why not? If not, what would your concerns be about these differences?

- What are your favorite creative pursuits or hobbies? How important are they in your life? Is it important to you to have a partner who shares some or all of these hobbies, or is it fine for her to have her own hobbies?

- What are your dietary habits? How important is it that your partner's diet be similar? If her diet is important to you, why?

- What is your usage of alcohol and drugs? How important is it that your partner's usage be similar?

- Are you a morning person or a night owl?

- If you hope to live together, are you a neat freak, super clean, "casual," or messy?

- Again, if you hope to live together, do you generally prefer quiet in your living space, or do you frequently play music or have the TV on?

Beyond The Two of You

- Do you envision having children in your ideal partnership? What's important in your vision of having children together, or being childless together?

- Do you envision having pets together? If so, what kinds, and how many? What's important to you about having pets together, or being petless together?

- Do you envision doing some kind of larger project together – e.g. volunteer work, political volunteering, or co-creating something?

Gender & Sexuality

- Where do you fall on a butch-femme or stud-femme scale, and what does this mean to you?

- If butch or stud/femme dynamics or roles are important to you, how would this play out in your ideal partnership?

- Do you define your sexual orientation as lesbian, queer, bisexual or something else? Would this be reflected in your ideal partnership in some way?

- Are you committed to monogamy, committed to poly-amory, or do you have a different vision (for instance, Dan Savage's concept of "monogamish," which means "largely monogamous but open to some exceptions.") Whatever your vision is, what's most important to you about this?

- How do you define sexual compatibility, and how would you know who is a sexually compatible partner for you? (e.g. how often you have sex, specific sexual activities, how long you spend having sex, etc.)

- How important is sex to you? How does this level of importance play out in your ideal partnership?

The Joy of the Rub – But Not Too Much Rub

These questions are a way for you to learn more about yourself and what's most important to you in a relationship. They're a starting point, not an end point. Some of them will identify crucial compatibility factors for you, while others may not feel important to you at all.

Being in a relationship with a unique, living, breathing individual – who will have her own hopes, dreams, fears, history and priorities – is an exciting process. And as we said before, your partnership will be co-created by both of you. This means that you won't get to have everything you think you want, exactly in the ways you think you want it. That would require being with a "Stepford Wife" or a blow-up doll rather than a real person.

Plus, getting everything you think you want might not even make you happy. Part of the joy of relationships is in the "rub," the places of friction, where you get to stretch and grow in directions you might never have imagined – that actually end up feeling good.

At the same time, your relationship is likely to be easier and more satisfying if you partner with someone whose values, needs, priorities and visions are similar enough to yours that there's common ground. And, knowing where you differ from the get-go will also help the two of you approach your differences with consciousness and compassion.

So the point of the questions above is not to make you rigid, or lead you to interrogate women on the first date to make sure they line up with everything you've outlined. But it *is* to help you get clear on what matters most to you.

In our ideal world, women might not whip out this kind of questionnaire on the first date, but you'd certainly keep these questions in your mind as you got to know the woman you were with. And within the first few dates, just in the process of spending time together, you'd learn what her answers would be to many of these questions – and you'd also think carefully about whether those answers meant she could be a good match for you, or not. We'll talk more about that process – which we call *assessment* – in Roadmap Week 12.

CHAPTER 13

Week 10:
Develop Your Dating Plan

✓ Explore the online and in-person options for meeting women, and the advantages, pitfalls, do's and don'ts of each method – and then chart your dating course.

Landmark: *Once you've completed this week's step, you'll have a dating plan that's effective and smart for your heart.*

How do I find her? That's one of the questions we hear most frequently. Since you've made your way to this point in the book, you should be much clearer about who she is, at least in terms of her qualities, her values and her vision. That will certainly make it easier to find her.

Sometimes, magic happens and the right woman just "shows up" once you're ready. However, we suggest you don't rely on magic. Instead, we recommend that you develop a dating plan, a systematic way to go about finding the woman you'll want to partner with.

Let's take a look at some of the most common ways of meeting women to date, the advantages and disadvantages of each, and how to choose.

Online Dating

Online dating is actually a misnomer, since the dating itself actually takes place offline. What we're actually talking about is how to meet women whom you want to date – and searching online for a prospective partner has some big pluses, as well as some potential pitfalls.

Using online dating sites gives you access to the profiles of thousands of women – and thousands of women can see your profile, too, if you post one. This has its pros and cons.

Pros of Online Approaches to Meeting Women

- If you live in an area where there aren't many lesbians, online dating solves that problem. You can easily meet women from all over the world, and when you meet someone with whom you're truly compatible, and lay a strong foundation first, one of you can eventually move to be with the other. (Of course, this is a huge step to take, and we encourage you to take a lot of time making a decision like this, and get some coaching in the process.)

- If you know exactly what you want in a relationship, online dating will save you a huge amount of time and effort. It would be very cumbersome to explain your vision to many women, one after the other, in person, but with online dating, you just post it in a profile.

- If you're an introvert, online dating is great because it doesn't require you to be out socializing in order to meet women.

- If specific things are important to you, a site may let you specify those. If not, you can do a keyword search to find women who've used that keyword in your profile.

- Online dating removes the awkwardness of catching someone's eye across the room or striking up a conversation with a stranger, and lets you focus on what's most important to you.

Cons and Cautions for Online Approaches to Meeting Women

- Some women are great at expressing themselves in writing; others are not. It's important to look beyond someone's level of writing skill (unless writing skill is actually important to you in a partner) to try to get a sense of the person underneath the words.

- Some women write profiles that are more a description of who they'd like to be than who they actually are. If you meet women online, you'll need to be conscious of assessing them to see if they really are who they say they are. (Of course, the same is true with meeting women offline.) Women can lie both live and online, but the anonymity of online ads makes it a bit more likely.

- Many women who aren't truly ready for a relationship – but want one anyway – post profiles online. (Of course, women who aren't really ready also attend live singles events, go to bars, etc. – but we've found that because posting an online ad or profile is so easy, it attracts an even larger number of women who are on the rebound or ambivalent about relationships. So again, this is something to screen for.)

- It's rare, but it does happen: men or teenagers can pose as adult women in online ads. Straight women can pose as lesbians; coupled women can pose as single. The best way to screen for any of these situations is to move fairly quickly from emails or texts to a face-to-face meeting, or a video chat if you're not in the same area. If someone you've met online is at least a phone or video chat. If you're in contact with someone who's unwilling to move to phone or video chat after a few emails back and forth, we'd encourage you to discontinue contact.

- When reaching out to women online, it's very important not to take their responses – or lack of response – personally. The woman whose profile you're responding to is a total stranger. Any failure to respond may have absolutely nothing to do with you. She might have met someone already, she might have gotten back together with her ex, she might not be checking that email account, she might be busy… there are many possible reasons for a lack of response.

- Similarly, it's important not to get invested in the idea of a relationship with someone, or build up fantasies about her in your head, just on the basis of her profile. Remember, it takes time to get to know someone and find out if you're truly well-matched. (Of course, this applies to offline dating, too.

- If you're not out of the closet, online dating can expose you – though in general, most people who'd see your profile would be other lesbians or queer women.

- If you have a profession that requires confidentiality, online dating can be awkward. For instance, if you're a therapist, you might feel uncomfortable posting a profile because your clients might see it. Some therapists get around this problem by posting profiles without clearly identifiable head shots of themselves, and being cautious about the profiles they respond to.

Despite all of these cons or areas to be cautious about, we are big fans of online dating. We believe it's almost always the best way to find what can otherwise seem like the proverbial "needle in a haystack" – a woman who's truly right for you.

But then, we ourselves met through Michelle's Craigslist ad, so we might be biased.

Offline Dating

Some of the most common offline approaches to meeting women include:

- Joining Meetup groups (www.meetup.com) for lesbians or queer women in your local area, and attending events. Alternatively, you can join Meetup groups based on your other interests, though depending on where you live, there may or may not be many lesbians in attendance. You can also start a Meetup group yourself.

- Engaging in activities you love – hiking, sports, the arts, or whatever else interests you – and hoping to meet women at them.

- Going to lesbian or feminist events, concerts and festivals.

- Going to lesbian speed dating events, if you live in an area that has them.

- Asking friends and others in your social circle to introduce you to single women they know, whom they think might be a good fit for you.

- Going to lesbian/gay bars or coffeehouses.

- Cruising the organic produce aisles of your local independent supermarket (we've actually heard women talk about meeting this way, though it may only work in locations with lots of lesbians, like the San Francisco Bay Area.)

As with online dating, offline dating – or offline approaches to meeting women – has both pros and cons. Here are some we're aware of.

Pros of Offline Approaches to Meeting Women

- You get to see someone in the flesh from the get-go – so you can both assess your level of attraction to her, and also see how she moves, what her voice sounds like, what she really looks like, and how it feels to be in her presence.

- You'll know for sure she's not a man or a teenager (though you won't know for sure if she's single, and you may not be able to tell what her sexual orientation is.)

- If you meet someone through a shared interest, you'll know you have that interest in common.

- If you meet someone through a friend or acquaintance, they may be able to vouch for her in some way (though unless they know both you and her really well, that probably won't count for much.)

- Many women prefer the idea of meeting someone offline because it feels more "organic" and natural – although this is changing rapidly.

Cons and Cautions for Offline Approaches to Meeting Women

- It's much harder to meet a substantial pool of women in your age range this way, compared to online.

- You're limited to women in your own geographic area, in most cases.

- You won't know – unless or until you engage her in deep conversation – whether she shares any of your vision and values. This makes offline dating much more time consuming and, often, much more frustrating.

- You may get distracted by her physical attributes and find it harder to focus on what matters most to you.

- It can be harder for shy women to strike up a conversation in person than online.

As you can see, the list of both pros and cons of offline approaches to meeting women is much shorter. The truth is, unless you live in an area with a lot of lesbians and are extremely social, you'll probably have trouble finding women to date using offline means alone. This leads many women to feel a sense of scarcity about the pool of potential partners available to them – which in turn can lead to settling for a relationship that isn't really what you want, or just giving up.

We'd rather not see either of those things happen. From our work, we know that there are many thousands of women out there looking for each other, and we think it makes a lot of sense to broaden your sense of potential by looking online. It's more efficient, it's more specific, and it creates much more possibility in your dating life.

Reasons Why Women Don't Use Online Dating

Some women have told us that they are disappointed when so few women respond to their messages, and that has turned them off from dating online. Some women have told us they feel intimidated by the prospect of writing an online profile. Some are afraid they don't look good enough in their photos. Some feel vulnerable and exposed at the thought of posting such personal information online. Some are afraid of being contacted by women they're not interested in, or even by mentally unbalanced people.

We understand all of these concerns. Yet we still believe the advantages of searching for a partner online far outweigh the risks and disadvantages. Yes, it takes some awareness to skirt the pitfalls – but that's true with offline approaches to meeting women, too.

If You Choose To Meet Women Online...

We'd suggest the following guidelines for writing your profile:

- Be clear and specific about what matters most to you – both in your life, and in a relationship.

- Tell little stories or give examples to show who you really are. For instance, if you just spent the day helping friends move, or weeding your garden, or babysitting for your grandchildren, or out at a protest march, talk about that.

- Present yourself honestly, and also positively. Be authentic, but don't reveal painful aspects of your past unless they've become a positive aspect of who you are (for instance, if you're an abuse survivor who now runs groups to help other abuse survivors heal.)

- If there's anything about you or your life that you fear may be a "negative" in other womens' eyes, we suggest being upfront about it in your profile, but only after several paragraphs in which you've described other aspects of yourself and your life. This will let you weed out women who would reject you for that quality, while also presenting a fuller picture of yourself for women who might not initially think they want a partner with that quality – yet may be open, once they've been won over by other aspects of who you are.

- Your primary photo is probably the most important part of your profile. Research shows that the primary photo should have a genuine smile, and a slight tilt of the head. You also might ask a friend – or hire a professional – to take photos of you engaged in activities you love. That way your photos will not only show your features, but also reveal important aspects of who you are. For instance, if you love children, show yourself with kids. If you love hiking, post a photo or two of yourself on a trail. If you're a gardener, post photos of yourself holding up a prize tomato, or working in your yard. Research shows you should be close to the center of these photos.

- If writing and punctuation are not your strong suit, ask a skilled friend – or hire a professional – to clean up your profile so you can make a better impression. This isn't being deceptive; you'd do the same thing if you were writing a resume, so why not do it for an online profile? In other words, your self-presentation is worth taking seriously.

- Describe the specific positive attributes of the woman you seek, rather than saying what you're *not* looking for. If you feel you need to say "No…" (as in, No butches, No femmes, No smokers, No heavy drinkers, etc.) keep it to a minimum.

- Describe your relationship vision – e.g. "In my ideal relationship, my partner and I would live together in the country with goats and chickens," or "In my ideal relationship, my partner and I would co-parent several children." Don't be afraid of "ruling women out" by describing what you want. If they don't want the same thing, it's *good* to rule them out. There are many thousands of women online, so there really isn't a scarcity issue.

If online dating still feels scary to you, we'd suggest you consider getting some support or coaching to help you feel more comfortable, and to approach it in a way that's smart for your heart.

Of course, you don't *have* to be open to meeting women online. You can choose against it. But we believe that if you're serious about finding a partner who shares your vision and priorities, it's by far the best way to go.

Look at it this way. If you wanted to buy a very specific item – say, a green plastic inflatable raft with a dolphin on it – you might spend days driving all over town, checking every store around, and still not find what you wanted. But if you did a quick Google, Amazon or Ebay search for "green inflatable raft dolphin," you'd find one quickly. (For fun, I just searched by that term and saw some great-looking dolphin rafts.)

Of course, searching for a partner with whom you can co-create a life *is* much more complicated than searching for a specific item to buy. Yet some of the same principles still apply. Instead of searching Google, Amazon or Ebay, you'll conduct your search on Match.com, OKCupid, or one of the many smaller lesbian dating sites. But you can still enter your search terms, and still be much more likely to find the right partner than if you rely on offline methods alone.

Whether you choose offline or online methods of meeting women, we'd suggest that you take this search as seriously as you'd take a job search. It can feel vulnerable to announce so clearly to yourself – and to the world – that you want a partner and you're actively seeking one. But it's also a powerful place to stand.

And if you've done the other work outlined in this book, you're not seeking a partner out of a place of desperation, or because you're on the rebound. You're taking active steps to create the life you want. And personally, we feel that's something to be proud of.

Unconditional Love vs. Necessary Conditions

Many of us hold dear the idea of "unconditional love." It sounds great, doesn't it?

But the truth is, unconditional love is for gurus on mountaintops, who aren't actually having intimate relationships with any of the people whom they're unconditionally loving. It's a concept that is great in the abstract, but it doesn't have much to do with the realities of healthy human relationships.

To have a healthy human relationship, you get to set conditions. You *need* to set conditions. You might be able to feel compassion and appreciation for anyone, but that doesn't mean you can have a truly fulfilling relationship with just anyone. You can't.

So, whether you're looking for a partner offline or online, you should be clear about your conditions. Remember, you're not just looking for someone to whom you're attracted – or just someone who's attracted to you. You're not just looking for someone who's cute, or witty, or smart, or whose stories elicit tenderness from you.

To be able to have the long-term love you really want, you need to find someone with whom you'll truly be compatible over the long haul: someone who shares enough of your vision, and has enough skills – and/or has the commitment to developing enough skills – to make that vision a reality in a happy, healthy way.

She is out there, and you can find her. But to do so, you need to be clear on who and what you're looking for, and on your own necessary conditions.

CHAPTER 14

Roadmap Week 11: Outsmart Your Hardwired Brain Chemistry.

✓ Recognize the difference between limerence and love, and make good choices even when smitten by lust or infatuation.

Landmark: *Once you've completed this week's step, you'll be able to keep your body, brain and heart on the same conscious page.*

The Perils of Limerence

Let's assume you've been meeting women – online, offline, or both – and you've found someone who may be a good prospect. You like her. She likes you. Preliminary conversations suggest that you've got some things in common, and are looking for some of the same things.

You may have met in person, and felt a spark. Or you may just be communicating by email, text and video chat, if she's not local. Either way, that feeling of chemistry may be starting to develop – or maybe it's already hitting you full-force. *Zing.* You find yourself thinking about her a lot. Your heart pounds harder when you see you've got a message or text from her. *It's here.*

No, not the relationship you seek – not necessarily. It's still too early to know about that. What's here is: *limerence.*

As you may remember from Chapter 1, limerence is the technical term for "the honeymoon state," in which your brain floods with endogenous opiates (read: feel-good chemicals, your body's own equivalent of heroin) and you're high on "love."

Except that it isn't really love – it's lust, infatuation, attraction.

Limerence is fun – though it can also be scary, because it heightens fear of rejection. But when the limerence is mutual, it usually feels great – just like getting high can feel great. It's also dangerous, because these brain chemicals can fool you into thinking you've met your match before you even really know each other.

Our client Jenne had this experience. She answered an online ad, met a woman named Marge for coffee, and felt totally smitten. Jenne is a Women's Studies professor; Marge was a professor in another field. They both enjoyed writing, and had exchanged a few witty, intelligent emails before they even met. Jenne felt instantly attracted to Marge, and went home after their coffee date believing she'd found her next partner.

A few days later, Marge emailed Jenne to say she'd decided to try again with her ex-partner. Jenne was devastated. All the castles she'd been building in her mind – fantasy scenarios of the life she'd share with Marge – came crumbling down. She was a wreck. She cried for days.

Because Jenne had gone into limerence, she'd gotten way ahead of herself. She'd forgotten that she really didn't *know* Marge. She hadn't asked any questions about how long Marge had been single, or what Marge's relationship vision was. She didn't even know how Marge felt about *her.* She had let limerence take control – and it had steered her right into the wall.

In some ways, though, Jenne was lucky – because she was in limerence by herself. As intense as that experience was for her, limerence is even more intense when it's mutual, and when the women involved aren't just thinking about each other, but are actually being sexual.

Ruth: *My fastest plunge into limerence came on the heels of a big breakup. Because I'd been taking care of an ill partner for years, I hadn't gotten to have much fun – or much sex – in a long time. So it felt great when Lou and I started joking and flirting.*

The next day Lou began sending me sexually-charged instant messages (this was in the days before texting existed) and I was completely overcome by lust. The drive to go to bed with her completely took me over.

After three long days of sexual tension, Lou and I finally consummated our desire. The sex was great (how could it not be, after so much build-up?) and afterward, when Lou told me about her childhood, my heart filled with tenderness.

The challenge was that I was moving out of town two weeks later for a job 2000 miles away. Rashly, I invited Lou to move with me – and she agreed.

It took several months to put our plan into action, and by the time her moving day came, I already had qualms about joining my life with Lou's. But I thought it would hurt her too much if I told her what I was feeling, so I didn't. We spent thousands of dollars and enormous effort moving Lou cross-country, and once she got there, our relationship was a complete disaster. It took months to unravel the mess we'd made, and much longer to heal from the confusion and pain.

We've heard many similar stories from our coaching clients. Although couples of all sexual orientations are prone to limerence, we believe that in general, lesbians and queer women fall harder and faster – because both our biology and our acculturation predispose us to rapid bonding.

This explains the old joke, "What does a lesbian bring on the second date? A U-Haul."

Handling Limerence Wisely

So, if lesbians are so prone to limerence, and limerence can lead to such disasters, how can we handle limerence wisely?

Part of the answer lies in remembering what's happening. You can't prevent limerence from occurring, but you *can* recognize what's happening and try to compensate for it with your rational mind, rather than throwing yourself into it with abandon.

It's also possible to slow limerence down by avoiding sexually-charged conversation and physical contact in the early stages of dating. If attraction is present, the limerence will start up anyway, but at least it won't go full-force.

Yes, that means we do suggest waiting to have sex. This isn't for moral reasons – it's simply to spare your heart. If you know for sure that both you and the other person are able to enjoy each other in bed without getting emotionally involved, great. But most lesbians and queer women aren't so good at that – and some who think they'll be able to end up finding out the hard way that they can't.

We can't tell you exactly how long to wait. One month? Two? Six dates? Ten? But at a minimum, it's good to make sure before becoming sexual that 1) You both have the emotional skills and communication skills to handle whatever feelings come up, and 2) You're on the same page about what going to bed means and doesn't mean about your connection.

In other words, Limerence + Sex Does Not = An Instant Relationship.

We also suggest not making any major decisions about each other while you're in limerence. As a general rule, that means not moving in together, not moving to be nearer to someone, not getting engaged, and not making any other kind of big life plan together for a minimum of six months.

Because limerence feels so good, it's tempting to just let it take over. But if you've been through a disastrous relationship and breakup due to limerence – or more than one – it can help you temper yourself. If not, we hope you'll heed the cautionary tales in this book and temper yourself anyway. Although limerence is thrilling, remember what it is, and don't confuse it with what it's not.

Keeping Your Body, Brain and Heart On the Same Conscious Page

Instead of getting led astray by limerence, we recommend taking steps to keep your body, brain and heart on the same conscious page. This means paying close attention to what you feel throughout the process of dating – not just when you're physically in someone's presence, but also when you're emailing, talking on the phone, video chatting, texting – or even just thinking about her.

Often women say, "But I just want to listen to my heart." The problem is that what you're calling your "heart" may actually be your limerence.

On the other hand, even apart from limerence, your heart may indeed be focused on a woman's best qualities. You may be good at seeing her essence, the beauty of her spirit, and her potential.

Yet you can't have a relationship with someone's potential - you can only have a relationship with someone as she is today. So if who she is right now isn't a good fit for you, it's important to acknowledge that rather than hope or assume that she'll change, or that things will get better with time.

Part of your brain, and all of your body, may be flooded with the chemical high of limerence. Your heart may be flooded with desire and hope. Therefore, it's even more important to work for clarity with the rest of your brain.

The vast majority of women who emerge from difficult relationships report that the signs of that difficulty were there from very early on – they just didn't want to let themselves know what they knew, or pay full attention to what they saw. We understand – we both did the same thing ourselves in the past. But ignoring red flags is a way of setting yourself up for pain.

Michelle: *Early on in my relationship with Liz, we were having brunch at her house, and I said some small thing that deeply upset or triggered her. She got up from the table, went out to her back yard, and stopped speaking to me. I followed her, apologized repeatedly, and asked what was wrong, but she still wouldn't talk to me. Not knowing what else to do, I left.*

The next day she called me and acted as if nothing had happened. We never talked about it, and I thought, "Well, this won't happen once we get to know each other better."

In fact, the opposite was true. After Liz moved in with me, she regularly stopped speaking to me for hours or even days at a time. After these episodes, she was never able or willing to talk about what had happened. I began to walk on eggshells, afraid of setting her off. We stopped having sex. She didn't want to, but she wouldn't talk about that either. I just kept hoping things would change, but they never did – and eventually she broke up with me without explanation.

We hear many, many versions of stories like this from the women we work with. So our advice is to look very carefully, both early on and throughout the dating process, for potential signs of trouble. We're not suggesting you be paranoid – but we *are* suggesting you remain conscious and aware.

Flags: Red, Yellow, Green?

We talked about red flags, potential trouble signs, earlier, and now we want to go into more detail about how to assess just how red a red flag really is. Some of the potential red flags we list below may actually turn yellow or even green – if the woman involved can speak about the issue in a clear, self-responsible way that sits right with your gut, as well as the rest of you.

Other red flags, however, will remain red no matter what. For instance, if someone drinks and/or uses drugs daily, it's very unlikely she'll be able to show up as a self-responsible partner in intimacy – even if she acknowledges she's got a problem.

We're not suggesting you use this list of red flags as a way of judging other women. But we *are* suggesting you use it as a way of assessing them, and whether it would be healthy for you to be with them. It's great to accept each person as she is, but that doesn't mean you should form an intimate relationship with her.

We particularly suggest paying close attention if any of the following red flags are present:

- She's vague about when she and her ex broke up.

    Did they really break up? Are their boundaries mushy? Find out.

- She acknowledges having lied to, cheated on or abused past partner(s).

    Can she talk about what led her to do these things – and has she engaged in a deep process of self-exploration and healing since then? And is she committed to doing things differently in the future? If so, this may become a yellow flag – find out more, and observe carefully.

- She hasn't been in a relationship for many years.

  If she has consciously taken time off from relationships to do some growing, learning and healing, this can actually become a green flag. If she's been single for a long time because she's still angry or hurt about past relationships, the flag stays red – so, find out more.

- She's over 25, and she's never been in a relationship longer than a few months.

  Depending on what else she's been doing in her life, this may not be a red flag at all. It's perfectly legitimate to focus one's attention in other directions. However, if someone has never had a long relationship, it may mean that she lacks the skills to have one – so, find out more.

- She's barely spent any time single, or has had a great many short-term relationships.

  Many women who've spent very little time single don't have a solid sense of themselves, and this can make it hard to have a happy, healthy relationship. If she's had many short relationships, it may also be a sign that she creates drama in her relationships. On the other hand, if she can talk openly and honestly about what led to either of these patterns, and has done some work around them, this red flag may turn yellow.

- She wants to jump into a relationship with you immediately, and isn't willing to take things slow.

  Women who want to jump in too fast are often being driven by fear – fear of loneliness, fear of vulnerability, fear of rejection, or something else. But the even bigger red flag here comes if you make it clear that you want to take things slow, and she pressures you to do otherwise. Anyone who pressures someone she's just met is unlikely to be a respectful partner later on.

- She pressures you for sex.

  Again, if she pressures you for anything, *it's a bad sign. Respectful, self-aware, self-responsible women don't pressure each other.*

- She's financially unstable.

  Everyone goes through financial trouble at times, so this isn't necessarily a red flag. Find out how long she's been struggling, whether she's been more financially solid in the past, and how she intends to deal with her current circumstance. Also find out what her resources are, in terms of friends and family, so you can make sure she won't become dependent on you. (Once a healthy relationship is established, it's fine for partners to exchange financial as well as other kinds of support, if they so choose. But starting out a relationship with a pattern of dependence is not a good idea.)

- She doesn't have any friends.

  Again, assess the circumstances. If she's just moved to the area, it makes sense that she doesn't have any local friends – but does she have friends elsewhere? If she truly seems to have no friends in the world, it's probably because she either doesn't have the skills to develop emotional connections, or did something to sever those connections. So, pay close attention to how she communicates, how emotionally stable or volatile she is, and how self-responsible she is.

  With friends, more isn't necessarily better. If she's an introvert with one or two close long-time friends, great. If she's an extrovert with 50 "friends" who are really just passing acquaintances, that doesn't really count. What's important here is someone's track record of being able to get close and stay close in relationships where limerence is not a factor.

- She drinks or drugs to excess.

  Of course, "to excess" is a subjective phrase. Depending on your own history, you may think any drug or alcohol use is excessive – or you may feel fine with someone who regularly has a few drinks, or regularly gets high. In general, though, we believe that anyone who drinks or does drugs daily, drinks or drugs as a way of managing stress, or regularly goes on drinking or drug binges, will be impaired in her ability to have a happy, healthy relationship. Check out whether she gets anxious if she can't have her substance of choice, and whether she gets defensive when you ask her about her use of it. Both of these things will tell you a lot.

- She blames her previous partner(s) for whatever went wrong in their relationship.

  We all know what it's like to feel angry or hurt – but if she's still angry or hurt, she's not ready for a new relationship. And if she blames her partner for everything, it means she hasn't taken responsibility for the part she played in whatever took place between them – so she likely won't take responsibility with you, either.

- She's still angry at her past partner(s), and sees herself as a victim.

  See above.

- She can't take responsibility for her own feelings.

  See above.

- She gets defensive or avoidant when you talk about certain issues.

  If someone can't or won't talk about certain issues when you're dating, it's likely she won't talk about them once you're in a relationship, either – and having "off-limits subjects" doesn't make for easy, happy, healthy love. On the other hand, it's a good sign if she can simply say clearly that she doesn't know you well enough to talk with you about a given topic yet, and will be glad to talk about it later as your connection deepens. Check out her energy, as well as her willingness to disclose. There's a big difference between someone who has healthy boundaries, and someone who is unwilling to share or dive deep.

- She spends a lot of time talking about her last relationship.

  If she's still emotionally wrapped up in her last relationship, she's not ready for a new one yet. But if she talks about her last relationship as part of sharing what she learned and how she grew, changed or healed in that partnership, or since it ended, this red flag may change to yellow or even green.

- She still lives with or is very close with her ex.

  In some cases this may mean they haven't really parted yet, emotionally or energetically. On the other hand, this red flag can turn green if you sense that she has a truly clear, clean friendship or housemate relationship with her ex. Someone who has the maturity to create a lasting bond with a former partner may well have better relationship skills than someone who never speaks to her ex-partners. So this flag can be red, yellow or green, depending on the details.

- She spends a lot of time complaining… about anything or anyone.

  Negativity is a bad sign. For one thing, it's not much fun to be around. For another, it suggests that she's not taking responsibility for her own emotions.

- She spends most of the time talking, rather than listening to you.

  This may mean she doesn't have the skills to listen and be present with another person, or that she's self-absorbed or narcissistic. On the other hand, if it's only your first date, it might just mean she's nervous. In this case, we'd suggest you make a direct request to shift the conversational flow so that you can share more of yourself with her, and see what happens. For example, you might say, "I've really enjoyed learning more about you, but I'm noticing that I'd really like to get to tell you more about myself, too." Her response will tell you a lot. If she gets angry or defensive – or lets you start talking, only to interrupt you a minute later – the flag gets redder. If she says "Oh, of course, I'm so sorry, I talk a lot when I get nervous" and then listens to you attentively, the flag turns green.

- She acts distracted in your presence, and spends time texting or otherwise ignoring you.

  Again, we'd suggest making a direct request, and see what happens. Also, notice whether this is a frequent pattern. Don't rule someone out because she happens to be having a crisis at work that day. Just find out more.

- She says something mean to or about you, or to or about anyone else (including herself.)

  There's really no excuse for meanness. The only caveat here is that you need to make sure you're really listening cleanly, so you're not mishearing her. Ask yourself the Byron Katie questions: Is it true? Are you absolutely sure it's true? But if she is mean to you, herself or anyone else, then she doesn't have the compassion a healthy relationship requires.

- She says one thing, but her behavior is different (e.g. she says she's into open, honest communication, but she isn't forthright, and doesn't express her emotions.)

  Don't just listen to her talk; check out her walk, as well. People sometimes describe themselves as they wish they were, rather than as they actually are.

- She gets extremely reactive over something small, and it takes hours or days before you're able to clear the air again – or else she tries to move on as if nothing had happened, without ever clearing the air.

  This is a very bad sign – because it suggests that she doesn't have the self-responsibility or communication skills that a healthy relationship requires.

This list is not exhaustive. You may have run into other red flags. If so, add them to the list.

Now, remember that most of these red flags are "Proceed with Caution and Find out More" signs. Again, in assessing just how red a flag is, you need to take into account what she says, what she does, what your gut sense tells you, and how you feel in her presence.

If you're not sure whether you can trust yourself – for instance, if you've had a past pattern of "overlooking" abuse – we'd also suggest you ask someone you trust for their opinion, or contact us for some coaching.

If you do decide you want to stop seeing her, how should you handle it? And on the flip side, what should you do if you see enough green flags that you sense there may truly be potential between the two of you? Or what if you're not sure which way to go?

We'll talk more about all of these scenarios in the next chapter.

CHAPTER 15

Week 12:
Date, Communicate & Assess
(And Rinse, Lather, Repeat.)

✓ Skillfully navigate the first few dates, gracefully stop dating someone when necessary, and/or consciously deepen the connection when you choose.

Landmark: *Once you've completed this week's step, you'll be in the "dating driver's seat" – and you'll be a great driver.*

The End of the Roadmap – And the Beginning of the Next Journey

You're reaching the end of the 12-Week Roadmap – and if you've stuck with the process, you've done a lot of learning and growing by now.

1. Let's review what you've worked on so far:

2. You've examined and released negative beliefs about love – and unrealistically positive fantasies, too – and replaced them with beliefs that are congruent with the kind of relationship you actually want.

3. You've cultivated more self-love and self-compassion, and relinquished patterns of self-criticism.

4. You've recognized your part in co-creating whatever happened with your former partners, forgiven yourself, and made peace with the past.

5. You've practiced befriending your emotions and letting them move through you, without getting caught up in mental stories.

6. You've learned the basic principles of clean speech and clean listening, and have hopefully begun to apply them in your life.

7. You've explored the five steps of the SCORE Process, a powerful way to dismantle triggers and heal conflicts at their source, and have hopefully begun to make use of that process, too.

8. You've learned body-based techniques for working with fear, so it doesn't have to dictate your dating and relationship choices.

9. You've gained more understanding of attraction, chemistry and compatibility, and you now know the most important kind of compatibility to seek in a prospective partner.

10. You've created a clear vision of the relationship you want.

11. You've created a dating plan to help you meet a partner who's truly right for you.

12. You've learned how to avoid being led astray by limerence, and how to keep your body, brain and heart on the same conscious page.

What's next? Well, the process of consciously dating.

The Conscious Dating Process

Our definition of conscious dating is: *spending time with a potential romantic partner while remaining curious, open to both your observations and feelings, and loving yourself through the process.*

There's something about dating that brings out the 13-year-old in most of us. Even if you feel like a perfectly capable adult in the rest of your life, or most of it, dating may make you feel shy, awkward, scared, insecure, or anxious. This might lead you to feel tongue-tied – or to feel as if you have to talk non-stop.

You might feel as if you have to do particular things to entertain or take care of the woman you're with. You might find yourself energetically leaving your body, going on auto-pilot while feeling less than fully present.

If any of these feelings come up, remember what you've learned about *befriending your feelings* and *being loving and compassionate toward yourself.* You may want to spend some extra time consciously just letting yourself feel your feelings, doing the SCORE Process with yourself, and saying some extra Metta for yourself, too.

We strongly suggest reminding yourself of your conscious dating intention before each date: *My intention is to remain open to my feelings while spending time with _____, and to love myself through the process.*

And you may also want to use the Fear Melters. Do some oozing, wiggling, sumo posture or love-scooping before your dates, after your dates, or even *with* your dates, if you're really brave. (You can tell her what you're doing and invite her to Fear Melt along with you. Remember, she's probably as nervous as you are.)

(Of course, if you're not quite that brave, you can also excuse yourself mid-date, go to the bathroom, and do some Fear Melting there.)

The purpose of all these practices is to *keep you connected to yourself* during the dating process. There are a few important reasons for this:

1. When you remain connected to yourself, you'll be able to have a good time on the date, regardless of whether or not you connect well with the other person you're with.

2. You'll also be able to connect more authentically with the woman you're dating.

3. You'll be more able to be curious and observant.

4. And, you'll be able to observe what you're feeling in your body throughout the date – which will give you important information.

Sandy's Conscious Dating Story

Our coaching client Sandy – whose story we tell in more detail in Part III of this book – came to us with a history of being attracted to "edgy" women. When we asked what she meant by "edgy," it turned out that the women she was drawn to were often controlling or downright mean.

Sandy is an extrovert who has no trouble meeting people, so she was actively dating various women during our first weeks of coaching. First came Drew, then Yvonne, then Cassie. Sandy was attracted to each of them – but after learning and using the Metta practice, doing other self-love work, and spending more time noticing the sensations in her body, she recognized that what she had thought of as arousal was actually linked to fear.

In other words, when Sandy felt fear in the presence of someone she was dating, she responded by getting turned-on.

This was a real light-bulb moment for Sandy. She had felt a lot of fear as a kid – her mother had been abusive, and she had also been bullied at school. And in a very clever survival strategy, her body had learned to eroticize the feelings of fear, to make them more bearable.

Once she recognized what was happening, and breathed more deeply through it, Sandy broke up with Cassie and spent some time shifting her belief that she wanted or needed to be with an "edgy" woman. A month later, she met Nicole at a party, and found that she was able to feel a whole different kind of attraction to Nicole – an attraction that was still erotic, even though it emerged from feeling safe.

Logistics of Conscious Dating

In our ideal world, dating would always take place in person, because you can get so much more information about people that way. However, in the real world, you may also date by phone or video chat if you have busy schedules or don't near one another.

One caution: we strongly suggest not having any kind of substantial conversation via text. It's just too easy to misinterpret each other that way. Although you can learn a lot by phone or video chat, there's really no substitute for face-to-face time. We believe it's wise for women who are geographically separated to arrange to spend some significant chunks of time in the same physical locale before making decisions about their romantic future.

If you've met online but live near one another, we suggest meeting in person after just a few email exchanges or phone calls, at most. This gives you a chance to experience the connection in person, rather than risk building up a lot of fantasies about someone.

If you've met in person, you may have a better sense of her already, but of course, getting together one-on-one, and in a dating context, is quite different from being together at a group activity.

If you both like to walk, taking a walk together is a great alternative to meeting for coffee, tea or a meal. There's something more natural and less awkward about being in motion rather than planted across a table from each other, and exercising your body will also tend to keep you *in* your body, and keep you breathing.

If that's not feasible, meeting across a restaurant or café table for a first date is fine, but we suggest you vary the scene for a second date. Find something you both like to do – whether it's a movie, a concert, a political rally, playing miniature golf, going to the beach, ice skating, skiing, dancing, or painting pottery – and do it together. This gives you a more "real world" context in which to observe the person you're dating, and see how it feels to be in her presence.

Of course it's great when dating is fun, but it's even better in some ways if something goes "wrong," since you can get so much information that way. For instance, if you get caught in traffic, the movie you'd planned to go to is sold out, you have trouble finding each other at the crowded rally, or one of you falls at the ice rink, you can learn a great deal from observing how she responds – and how the two of you handle the challenge together. Are you both able to stay present, connected and compassionate toward yourselves and each other? If so, that's a great sign. But if one or both of you gets flustered, anxious, blaming or self-blaming, the most important thing is to see whether you're able to talk openly about it, either right then or later, once things have calmed down. If so, that too is a good sign. But if not, keep an eye on it.

If you live near one another, we also suggest visiting one another's homes early in the dating process. You can learn a lot about someone from seeing how she lives – and also seeing how she feels about having you come over.

Of course, you can also learn about yourself by seeing how *you* feel about having her come over – and seeing what happens when she does.

Ruth's Conscious Dating Story

My first date with Dina was at a big park with walking trails. As we walked, I noticed that I felt attracted to her and that there was something I enjoyed about being in her presence, but at the same time, there was something "off" about our conversation. For one thing, she talked a lot more than she listened. For another, most of what she said seemed to revolve around having felt wronged or victimized by other people in some way.

At this point I was midway into learning conscious dating skills. I knew more than I'd known in the past, but a lot less than I know today. So even as I took a mental note of the red flags, I decided there was enough promise to warrant inviting Dina to my house for dinner a few days later.

The night before Dina was going to come over, I dreamed I was dating a man who I knew was actually Dina (Dina was quite butch, so it wasn't too surprising that my dream turned her into a man.) But in the dream, the man had actually been my client, so I realized I shouldn't be dating him. Then something rather disastrous happened, and I fled the man's house and ran outside to my car. I was afraid my car wouldn't start, but it did, and gratefully I roared away.

This dream gave me pause, but I wasn't sure how to interpret it – so again, I just took a mental note.

At the appointed hour, Dina showed up at my house with a bottle of wine. Then she walked into my kitchen, set the wine down on the table, and announced, "I'm probably an alcoholic. I drink wine every night, and have for many years."

O-kay. Right then and there, I knew why my dream had represented her as a "client" – i.e. someone in need of help, rather than a peer – and why I had felt I had to flee from her/his house and get away.

Since she was already at my house, I didn't cancel the date. But after we finished dinner, I made it clear to Dina that I couldn't continue to date her. "I'm a healer, and my whole life is about healing. It just wouldn't make sense for me to date someone who is an alcoholic," I explained as gently as I could.

Dina didn't take kindly to this. In fact, she did everything in her power to convince me to change my mind. First she said that I had been drinking tea both times she'd seen me, and why was that any different from her drinking alcohol? Next she accused me of judging her. She said some other rather bitter things, too, before I got her out the door.

Whew. Disaster averted – though it wasn't quite over yet. Over the next couple of weeks, Dina continued to email me to try to get me to change my mind (and I continued to respond – so obviously, I was waffling a bit.) Her emails became very seductive. Basically, she started telling me what a great lover she was, and how much being with her would open me up in bed. I hadn't had good sex in quite a while, so I felt momentarily tempted. But then I came back to my senses and cut off our contact. (Now I see why, in the dream, I was at first afraid that my car wouldn't start – but then it did, and I drove away.)

Assessing the Women You Date (Or Consider Dating)

Hopefully your dating plan is bringing you into contact with enough women that you're not suffering from a sense of false scarcity – so you can truly assess each woman with compassionate clarity. Remember, this isn't about judging her, but it *is* about making conscious choices about what works for you. We call this process *assessment*.

Obviously, in order to assess the women you date, you need to keep the Red Flag list in mind. In my (Ruth's) story above, Donna waved many major red flags in the air – not only with her announcement that she was "probably an alcoholic," but also with the array of responses she had when I told her I didn't want to date her.

Although these red flags were pretty obvious, in earlier days I might still have ignored them, given both the chemistry between us, and the pressure Donna put on me. I might have told myself I wouldn't get involved with her, but then gone to bed with her just to "break my dry spell." If I had done that, I imagine we'd have fallen strongly into limerence, and I'd have found myself in a relationship despite my best intentions.

Let's take a look now at some of the other, less obvious red flags our clients have spotted – some which stayed red upon further exploration, others of which turned green.

Jill's Red-To-Green Flags Story

Our client Jill, 58, whose story is told more fully in Part III of this book, was excited but wary when she met Cherie, 60. One of the red flags she spotted early on was that Cherie wasn't working. Jill had saved a nest egg for herself, and was very clear that she didn't want to become someone's Sugar Mama.

"Cherie doesn't seem concerned about not working," Jill told us. "She seems to own her own house, and apparently a friend who died recently left her some money, too. But I don't like the idea that she's unemployed."

We encouraged Jill to find out more about Cherie's finances, and exactly why she wasn't working. "I can't ask her that." Jill said, aghast. "It's none of my business."

"Actually, Jill, it is your business, if you're considering getting into a relationship with Cherie," we assured her. Then we role-played ways she could find out more about Cherie's situation, without being invasive.

Jill did manage to get the question out, and found out that Cherie was a freelancer with plenty of work opportunities – and was also financially solid enough that she didn't really have to work.

"I don't know if Cherie will be okay with my skiing trips," Jill told us at her next coaching session. "Dani, one of my skiing buddies, is someone I briefly dated. Dating just wasn't the right fit for us, but Dani's a bit younger than Cherie, and Cherie has made a few comments that make me think she feels insecure."

Again, we encouraged Jill to talk directly with Cherie about what had happened between her and Dani, and also about how important it was to her that her partner be okay with her taking a few solo skiing trips a year. At her next coaching session, Jill reported with relief that Cherie didn't seem jealous any more, now that they had talked more fully.

On the other hand, our client Felice, 39, ran into red flags that got even redder as time went on. With our help, she realized she needed to disentangle herself from a woman she'd met after just one date.

Here's her Conscious Dating story.

Felice's Red-to-Redder Flags Story

When Clara answered Felice's personal ad, it sounded as if the two women might be a match to become "friends or more." They both loved the outdoors, and both were involved in similar progressive Christian-based churches.

On their first meeting, however, Clara, 37, told Felice that she was very serious about having a child, and had begun the process of trying to find a sperm donor. Felice, who liked Clara but didn't feel a strong click, felt clear that this meant they weren't a match for being romantic partners. She told Clara that she wasn't interested in co-parenting, but suggested they spend the rest of the hike exploring the possibilities of friendship.

Things seemed to go well on the hike, so Felice had Clara over to her house for a brief cup of tea afterward. She thought they were on the same page about becoming friends, so she was very surprised to get a long email from Clara the following day.

Clara wrote, After I left your house, I spent hours journaling and crying. I couldn't believe I'd met someone who seemed so perfect for me, but who didn't want to have children. I prayed to God for help.

This morning when I woke up, I had the answer. My desire to have children came from loneliness, and if we're together, that hole in my soul will be filled – so I really don't need to have children after all. I hope we can see each other again very soon.

Felice was taken aback. She hadn't really felt that she and Clara were a match, even apart from the issue of children. But she was also very concerned that someone who had been so serious about becoming a mother would do such an about-face after just one date.

"I don't like the idea that she would give up having children for me, when we don't even know what might happen between us," Felice told us.

We agreed. "The role of partners isn't to 'fill holes in each other's souls,'" we told her. "It sounds like she's trying to make you responsible for her emotional well-being."

When we asked Felice more about Clara's history, it turned out that at 37, she had never had a relationship that had lasted more than a few months. Although this isn't always a red flag, it seemed pretty red given Clara's other statements.

With our support, Felice gently but firmly told Clara that she didn't feel they were a match to continue dating, but she was still willing to explore being friends – as long as Clara was okay with the fact that that was all they'd be. She wasn't really surprised, though, when Clara said she didn't think she could handle that, given how strongly she felt toward Felice – so they agreed not to see each other again.

In some cases, it's hard to know for sure whether a red flag is truly red – or whether it might be yellow, or even green. In these cases, you need to make a judgment call. Again, this doesn't mean judging the other woman involved; it means judging for yourself whether it feels right to you to continue.

We suggest you listen to your gut – not your fear, not your rational mind, not your heart (which is too often focused on fantasy or on someone's potential), and certainly not the voice of limerence.

Nia's Red-to-Red Flag Story

When Nia, 45, agreed to meet Ginny for coffee, she didn't expect anything to come of it. Ginny lived out of state, but had previously lived in Nia's town, and said she planned to move back there soon.

They had only exchanged a few brief emails, so Nia didn't know much about Ginny – but in person, she was surprised by how attracted she felt. They had a lively conversation, which moved quickly to a lively flirtation. Ginny said some things which made it sound as if they'd be highly sexually compatible. Feeling intrigued and turned-on, Nia agreed to meet Ginny again the next day.

Over coffee, Ginny had mentioned that she was in recovery, but Nia hadn't asked the details. On their second date, Ginny explained that she had been addicted to crack. Although she'd had a high-level job and made good money, when things fell apart in her relationship she went full-force into her addiction, eventually becoming jobless and homeless.

"Wow." Nia said. "How long ago was that?"

"Three years ago."

"So, when did you get clean?"

"Two and a half years ago. That's why I live out of state now. I moved because I needed to get away from the people I was doing drugs with."

Nia felt somewhat relieved. Two and a half years seemed like a pretty solid amount of recovery.

"So you've been clean since then?" she asked, just to be sure.

"No," Ginny admitted. "I actually moved back here a year later, so I could be closer to my kids. But I was dating someone, and when she broke up with me, I went back to using. So I moved away again, and got clean again. This time I've really learned my lesson."

"So how long have you been clean this time?" Nia asked, noticing that there was a tight feeling in her throat. She realized she felt scared.

"Eleven months," Ginny said. Nia wasn't sure what to say. The silence hung in the air between them.

Finally Nia found words again. "I need to tell you something. My father is an addict, and so is my sister. So your history makes me pretty nervous."

"Oh," said Ginny. "I didn't know that."

"Yeah," said Nia. "I'm sorry, but I think I just wouldn't feel comfortable dating you. It's not you, it's me. I mean, I hear you about being committed to staying clean. It just hits too close to home for me."

"I wish you felt differently," Ginny said. "But I guess I have to accept your decision."

Because she was following the principles of conscious dating, Nia listened to her body signals, which told her she felt anxious and scared. And because she was aware of red flags, she decided that this fear wasn't just something for her to "melt," it was something she wanted to listen to.

"I felt especially nervous," Nia told us later, "Because Ginny's addiction and relapse were both triggered by relationship issues. If I dated her, I'd be terrified that if anything went wrong between us, she'd go back to using yet again." We told her we understood.

"On the other hand, she's been clean for eleven months," Nia continued, second-guessing herself. But then she added, "But it's *only* been eleven months."

Our minds can go back and forth like this forever – but Nia's gut had already given her answer.

Will Ginny stay clean this time? Maybe. Would Nia and Ginny have a good relationship, if Ginny stayed clean? Maybe, again. It was too soon to know. Ginny's history certainly contained some big red flags; on the other hand, her level of honesty about her history – and her maturity in accepting Nia's response – are both green flags.

It's impossible to know whether Nia's choice led her to avert a disaster, or cut a great potential partner out of her life. But crack addiction and relapse are very serious, and given her family history, Nia was particularly sensitive to the issues. So she definitely made the choice that was right for her.

Truth in Dating

As you can see, we encourage truth in dating. This means clearly, directly expressing your concerns, stating your feelings, and asking questions when you need to know more about something the woman you're dating has said, or hasn't said.

Many women feel uncomfortable being so direct. Some, like Jill, feel that asking straightforward questions is "none of their business." Others are just afraid of making the other person feel put on the spot, interrogated or interviewed.

We've also found that most of our clients are just as afraid of making someone else feel rejected, as they are of feeling rejected themselves. As women, many of us have a pattern of taking responsibility for other peoples' feelings. At its worst, this pattern can actually lead women to stay for years in relationships they don't want to be in, simply because they don't want to hurt the other person.

We understand this pattern – we've lived it out ourselves. I went ahead with moving Lou, a woman I barely knew, across the country to be with me even though I had qualms about it, because I "didn't want to hurt her." And Michelle stayed for years in an abusive relationship, because she'd promised her partner she would stay – and again, she didn't want to hurt her.

Women, we need to get over this. *You* are every bit as important as whoever you're dating. *Your needs, wants and feelings count.*

Remember the principle we discussed in the chapter on the SCORE Process: You are 100% responsible for your own feelings, and 0% responsible for anyone else's feelings.

You are also 100% responsible for the choices you make – and those choices determine whether you'll end up alone, in a bad relationship, or in the kind of happy, healthy relationship you really want. *Your relationship destiny is in your hands.* Hold it wisely.

Clear Communication

Here are examples of how the women we've described communicated with their dates.

Ruth to Donna: "I've enjoyed spending the evening with you, but I don't want to date you. I can't date an alcoholic."

Jill to Cherie: "I know you might say it's none of my business, but I was wondering if you could tell me more about your work and money situation. I don't need to know how much money you have, I just need to know we're both on the same page about being financially independent."

Felice to Cherie: "Wow, I didn't realize you were committed to having children. I'm very clear that I don't want children, so I guess that means we're not a fit to date."

Jill to Cherie: "I really want to make sure you understand that Dani and I are just friends. We tried dating and it didn't work, so there's nothing like that between us. But I do like going on skiing trips with her. I'd like to date you but I just want to make sure you wouldn't feel weird about my going on ski trips with Dani."

Nia to Ginny: "I'm sorry, but I think I just wouldn't feel comfortable dating you. It's not you, it's me. I mean, I hear you about being committed to staying clean. It just hits too close to home for me."

In each of these cases, the women involved communicated something important, something they needed to say.

In some cases, the conversations went well. In other cases, they didn't. Communicating clearly doesn't guarantee that the other person won't feel hurt or upset, or that she'll respond maturely. *But it's important to do it anyway.*

Beyond The Flags: How Can You Know If She's Right?

We have several answers to the question of how you can know if the woman you've met might truly be a compatible partner for you, someone with whom you can co-create a happy, healthy long-term relationship.

One answer is that this is something you can only know over time – ideally a year or more. (We would absolutely suggest not making any major relationship decisions, such as getting engaged, moving to be closer to each other, or moving in together, sooner than six months – and a year is better.) You need to be with someone and observe her – and observe yourself in her presence – many different times, and in many different kinds of situations, to learn whether the two of you have "the right stuff" together.

Another part of the answer, of course, is to see how well you match up in terms of compatibility. Remember, there are three levels of compatibility, and all are important, but level 3 is most important of all. So, ask yourself:

- Do we share enough interests and lifestyle factors in common?

- Do I enjoy being around her, and feel a sense of rapport and attraction?

- Is her relationship vision similar to mine, and does she have the skills to manifest it? In particular, is she committed to learning, growing and working with her own "stuff" self-responsibly?

And the third part of the answer is that it's important to look closely at who she *is* – in other words, not just the talk she talks, but the walk she walks. Some women may say they're committed to growth and self-responsibility, but when the proverbial sh** hits the fan, they turn blaming, critical and manipulative, or just aren't willing to work with their triggers. On the other hand, there are women who may not speak the same personal growth language you do, yet may still have a lived commitment to clear, clean communication and owning their own feelings.

Of course, you also have to look closely at who *you* are in the relationship. Are you, too, showing up in your full commitment to growth and self-responsibility? Are you doing the SCORE Process with your triggers, and speaking and listening cleanly? Before accusing someone else of "not walking her talk," do make absolutely sure you're walking your own.

No one does this perfectly, of course. And as we often say, you don't have to be perfect – you just have to be ready. To us, "being ready" means having a strong commitment to the principles of self-love, self-compassion, clean communication and self-responsibility, so you can show up with your wisest self, rather than speaking or acting from triggers.

We have a personal story about this. Early on, something happened that almost stopped our own relationship from going forward – and then we had a conversation that shifted everything, and that showed us we were both ready.

Ruth & Michelle's Almost-Ending

Ruth: *Michelle and I had been dating for about two months, and I liked her a lot, but I wasn't sure she was "the one." Sex hadn't really clicked between us yet, and I had some concerns about that. Meanwhile, I could tell that she was falling for me, and that scared me. A lot.*

I had a painful history of feeling like I broke women' hearts. I'd left my long-term partner Gladys after seven years, and I knew Gladys had never fully gotten over it. I'd also been the one to end most of my other relationships, and felt a lot of guilt about how much pain I'd caused, even though I knew I had needed to leave.

So, the more I thought about it, the more I thought it might be better for me to just break up with Michelle sooner, rather than getting more deeply involved and hurting her more later.

She'd invited me over for dinner, and I felt racked by ambivalence. Should I still let her cook me dinner, even though I was thinking of ending our brief relationship? When during the evening should I tell her? I finally decided to go, but be honest, even at the risk of creating a scene.

I was very nervous, but I knew I wanted to be as open and vulnerable with Michelle as I could. Our connection thus far had been deep enough that I felt she deserved that. So, on my way out the door, I scooped up the bird wing from a blue jay my cat had caught and killed a few months earlier. I loved blue jays; I'd felt terribly sad about the bird's death, and had saved its wing as a symbol of beauty and vulnerability. As I drove to Michelle's house, I prayed for help in speaking clearly and with compassion.

When I got to Michelle's place, she showed me a video she'd been making, and we chatted for a while. Then I got up my courage, got out the bird's wing, and showed it to her. I told her I'd brought it to help me remember both her vulnerability, and my own. Then I began, "There's something I've been feeling that I need to tell you about..."

Michelle listened attentively. When I had finished my brief speech about being afraid of breaking her heart, she said simply, "I'm so moved by your courage and honesty. And our connection has been such a gift to me. Even if it ended right now, that would still be true."

I felt deeply relieved when I heard her words and felt her calm, open energy – and in response, my heart opened right back up again in my chest. Her response was what made me feel able to continue seeing her, and eight years later, it was that same calm, open quality that made me feel able to say Yes when she asked me to marry her.

I'm so glad I took the risk to speak truthfully that night.

Now, that's Ruth's side of the story. But how did it feel to Michelle to hear that the woman she'd been seeing for just two months – and, yes, had strong feelings for – was considering ending their relationship?

Michelle: *I did have an emotional reaction to what Ruth said. I remember feeling some fear, disappointment and sadness. Of course we hadn't yet invented the SCORE Process, but I think I must have done a version of it very quickly in that moment. So I felt my feelings and acknowledged them to myself - I didn't push them away – but at the same time, I recognized that they weren't what I wanted to bring to the forefront.*

And even as I felt the fear and sadness, I was also blown away by the vulnerability Ruth had shown – and that was what I really wanted to be with, because it felt like a gift.

This isn't something I would have been able to do earlier in my life. Ten years earlier, I might not have said much to Ruth, because I tended to be more the kind who'd withdraw to lick her wounds. But it would definitely have sent me into my old story about being broken, defective and unlovable.

But that night, that didn't happen. I think it's partly because of the year I'd spent doing Metta, and also partly because Ruth was so present and honest. That really opened the door for me to be present, too, and respond from my most open-hearted and wise self.

Going from the Roadmap to the Road

We hope these stories and examples have given you a sense of what's possible when you choose to date consciously – when you spend time with a potential romantic partner, cultivate curiosity, observe her and yourself, and feel your feelings and love yourself through the process.

Dating a real person is always complex and multifaceted, and whoever comes into your life, there will probably be questions and feelings you didn't anticipate, triggers you haven't felt in a long time, and all manner of fears, doubts and hopes.

That's all as it should be – and actually, as it has to be, since dating and relationships are deeply emotional processes. But along with the inevitable vulnerability and uncertainty, we hope you'll have a good time, too. As we said earlier, we believe that when you're dating consciously, every date can be a good date – whether you feel well-matched with the other person involved, or not – because you're being good company *for yourself* throughout the process.

Each interaction with a woman you're dating, or a woman you might like to date, gives you a chance to learn more about yourself, get clearer about what you want, practice your clean listening and communication skills, and exercise self-love and self-compassion – regardless of what else does or doesn't happen.

But if your dream is to create deeply fulfilling, lasting love, we wish that for you, too! We know you can get there. *She is out there.* And again, you don't have to be perfect to find her, or to create an amazing life with her. You just have to be ready!

In the final section of this book, we'll share more true-life stories with you to give you even more inspiration for the journey.

PART III

True Stories

Ruth's Note:

In this section, you'll get to read some of my own "True Disaster" stories — relationship traumas that would never have happened at all, or would have played out very differently, if only I had known then what I know now.

We'll also tell you more about the challenges some of our clients have faced and overcome, so you can celebrate with them and learn from their transformation.

Finally, I'll describe how Michelle's and my years of relationship disasters led us into a marriage more amazing than we could ever have imagined.

We got here. And you can, too!

CHAPTER 16

If Only I Had Known...
Disaster Story #1

Too Hot, Too Cold or Just Right: The Saga of PAP and PEP

"On days when we don't see each other, I want to talk for at least an hour on the phone," my new girlfriend Emily told me firmly.

We'd only been dating a few weeks, although we'd known each other for several months. I'd felt a strong attraction, a sense of recognition, the moment I first saw Emily. I found out later it was mutual.

On the first weekend we spent together, we went camping "as friends," and I slept in my own tent. But the first night, we stayed up very late, first talking and then going silent to gaze into the fire's coals. Though we didn't touch, even the proximity of our arms felt highly charged.

Emily was cute, she was crazy about me, and there was definitely chemistry. And she appeared to be completely available, unlike my last girlfriend. So what was stopping me?

Well, there were plenty of good reasons not to take the plunge. One was that I'd only been out of my last relationship – an intense,

passionate connection with a very long, messy, drawn-out ending –
for a few months.

Another was that I knew Emily drank wine every night. I didn't
exactly think she was an alcoholic, but the dependency made me
uncomfortable, and so did the pain I sensed it was masking. Emily
came on strong, but her vulnerability was also very apparent to
me. It was both appealing – "This woman will really let me get
close to her." I thought – and frightening.

After that weekend, I emailed my good friend Renee a list of
all the reasons why Emily and I should remain just friends. A few
days later, I reversed my position, deciding that it had just been
my fear getting in my way. Once again I emailed Renee, this time
explaining that I'd realized how perfect Emily and I really were for
each other.

That flip-flop should've been a clue to me that something was
not quite right. But I wasn't paying attention. I didn't want to pay
attention. I wanted to be in love. And I had convinced myself that
Emily was right for me after all.

But now, just a few weeks later, things weren't going so well.
I had never before had a girlfriend set an explicit rule about how
much we should talk. It made me feel claustrophobic.

The funny thing was, if Emily hadn't been insisting that we
talk on the phone for an hour a day, I might even have wanted to
talk on the phone for an hour a day. But having her insist on it
made me feel controlled and suffocated.

"And even when we're not talking, I want to be able to feel you
thinking about me," Emily continued. "Sometimes I feel you get
distant. I don't like that. There shouldn't be any distance in a relationship. I want to feel you energetically holding me all the time."

Uh-oh. An alarm bell was sounding inside me. "But what about
having healthy boundaries?" I protested. I was already working on

my Ph.D. in Transpersonal Psychology, so I'd read and heard a lot about boundaries.

"There shouldn't be any boundaries once you're in a relationship. You just don't know what real intimacy is. Your other girl-friends were scared of it, and so are you. But I'm not."

I couldn't deny that there had been problems in my past relationships. The truth was, I'd mostly been in Emily's position, trying to wheedle, demand or persuade my girlfriends to get closer to *me*. It was a strange shift to be on the other side.

I soon found that I was not looking forward to my mandatory daily phone calls with Emily. What was wrong with me?

I'd always thought of myself as someone who needed plenty of time alone. But Emily chalked that up to my sexual abuse history. "You just haven't felt safe being truly intimate before," she told me.

Who was right, Emily or me? And, more to the point, what were we going to do about it?

Power Struggles Over Closeness and Distance

Lesbians and queer women often fall into these types of power struggles. Whose experience do you identify with, Emily's or mine? Or have you, like me, occupied both positions at different times, or in different relationships?

After a week or two on the receiving end of Emily's requirements, I had much more sympathy for my ex-lovers (whom I had often prodded for more closeness.) I also realized that Emily's demands were actually killing off my feelings for her. I was losing any desire to see or be with her at all.

This made me feel terrible, and terrified. How could I hurt her that way? And how could I have felt so strongly drawn to her, and then gone so cold? What was wrong with me?

In my past relationships, when I'd been in Emily's role, I'd felt certain that I was in the right. I saw myself as the one who was more available for healthy closeness, and lamented the fact that I often seemed to pick such unavailable women.

Now, with frightening clarity, I realized that if my only two alternatives were to be chasing after someone or pushing someone away, I'd rather be chasing. Being in a nearly-constant state of longing felt bad to me, but feeling strangled, controlled and invaded felt even worse.

Fortunately, those are *not* the only two alternatives. But I didn't know that at the time.

In the Goldilocks fairy tale, Goldilocks samples two bowls of porridge – one too hot, one too cold – before finding the third bowl that is "just right." Yet I wondered whether that "just right" intimacy was even possible. Was it simply a matter of dumb luck, finding someone who happened to have intimacy needs and wants identical to my own? How would I ever do that?

When I looked around, I saw many couples in which this same dynamic seemed to play out. Almost always there seemed to be a "pursuer," and someone who got pursued. And when I asked, I learned that I wasn't the only person who had occupied different roles in different relationships.

Clearly, then, these patterns weren't fixed aspects of our personalities. Or rather, the potential for *both* patterns, wanting more closeness and wanting more distance, existed in all of us. This fit with what I was learning in school about attachment theory. It was a relief to realize that my experience wasn't unique, though I still didn't know what to *do* about it.

The End of The Power Struggle – And The Relationship

A few days later, feeling completely pushed against the wall, I ended my relationship with Emily. We'd been seeing each other for less than a month. She raged, begged, pleaded and tried hard to convince me I was wrong. Then she called me dozens of times, leaving angry and then sobbing phone messages.

I understood what Emily was going through. When Sarah had broken up with me a few years before, I hadn't called her dozens of times, but I had certainly wanted to. And in a different way, using more psychologically nuanced language, I had worked just as hard to convince Sarah that she was making a mistake, and to pressure her to change her mind.

When Emily's calls finally stopped, I felt a little like someone who had survived a tornado. It took me a long time to feel ready to date again – and years more before I finally understood what had actually happened.

Here's what I know now. Emily and I had gotten caught in a dynamic that we now, in Conscious Girlfriend, call "The Drama of PAP and PEP." Unfortunately, it's a very common drama between lesbians – but it doesn't have to be, once you know how to use the SCORE Process to work with it.

The Drama of PAP and PEP

PAP stands for "Primal Abandonment Panic," and we've all got it, though some of us get triggered into this panic more easily than others.

We have PAP because human infants are born tiny and helpless. Without the attention and care of someone older and more capable, we would quickly die. Therefore, we are biologically programmed to go into panic if our caretaker(s) abandon us, or if we *even believe we are at risk* for being abandoned.

This panic doesn't just get set off by physical abandonment. Infants are also extraordinarily sensitive to the presence or absence of emotional attunement – because the less emotionally attuned our caretakers are, the more likely they may be to abandon us.

Some of us grew up with parents who were actively neglectful or abusive. But even if that wasn't the case, none of us got all of our needs met the moment we experienced them. It simply isn't possible. So we are all prone to re-experiencing this state of Primal Abandonment Panic, or PAP.

This is why even highly capable, independent adults can go into an emotional and physiological state of panic that actually feels life-threatening when we feel abandoned by someone with whom we've bonded. And because lesbians bond so quickly and intensely, we may be even more prone to PAP and PEP dramas than other kinds of couples are.

By the way, this doesn't mean there's something wrong with lesbians. PAP and PEP are simply the shadow side of our amazing ability to get close. Lesbians can have the most amazing, deeply intimate relationships on the planet! But we have to watch out for getting blindsided by limerence *and* by PAP and PEP.

PEP stands for Primal Engulfment Panic, and it's PAP's opposite. It exists in each of us because we were not only biologically programmed to merge with our mothers as infants, but also to individuate – to separate from them – when we reached the age of about two.

And because individuation, becoming a separate person, is just as important to human development as getting taken care of in infancy, we're just as prone to PEP as we are to PAP. If you've ever felt intensely suffocated or strangled by a relationship, or, in a more extreme case, felt as if your feelings for your girlfriend suddenly seemed to dry up or disappear when she got too clingy, you were probably in PEP's grip.

Again, some individual women are more likely to go into PAP; others tend more toward PEP, and some of us lucky ones, me included, tend toward both.

If you're highly susceptible to both PAP and PEP, your inner world can feel like quite a circus, and lead to your giving your partner very different messages depending on which state you're in. "Come closer, come closer. Whoops, not *that* close. Get back. Get out of my space. Wait, where'd you go? Come closer. No, no, not *that* close. Whoa. Back up. Give me room to breathe. Uh-oh, you're too far away. Come baaaaaack…."

It's easy to see what a mess this can create in intimate relationships. Often one person's PAP triggers the other person's PEP, which is what happened with Emily and me. Because Emily's PAP came up so quickly, within just a few weeks of our involvement, I wasn't yet deeply bonded to her. That's why my PEP led me to end the relationship. But in many couples, the battle of PAP and PEP goes on for years, keeping them locked in cycles of drama, confusion and heartache.

Often couples switch off; after the partner in PAP goes into despair and withdraws, the partner in PEP feels safe enough to re-initiate contact – and then the whole cycle, or a variation, plays out again and again.

No wonder I, like Goldilocks, was always encountering relationship "porridge" that was too hot or too cold.

Handling PAP & PEP

Since we are all prone to both PAP and PEP, and since both can wreak such havoc in our intimate relationships, what's the solution?

The first step is to recognize what's going on. The truth is, we all have a deep need for closeness – and we all have a deep fear of *too much* closeness. We all need separateness, too – and we also all fear having *too much* separateness. Our PAP and our PEP are at the root of those fears, and often lead us to attempt to amputate or truncate one half of our needs (or our partner's needs) or the other. But this is not sustainable over the long haul.

To really sustain intimacy, we need to be able to tolerate deep connection, and then flow in a natural rhythm into our separate selves again… and then flow back together, and then apart, over and over again. This is the dance of real intimacy. But in order to do it, we need to learn how to manage both our PAP and our PEP.

Acknowledging our PAP and PEP, first to ourselves and then to our partners, is the first step, and creates more room for our adult brains to have a say. Then when the mental and physiological distress signals go off, both we and our partners will understand what's happening and why. When we stop struggling – and stop pathologizing ourselves and each other – we're in a much better position to navigate both partners' needs for closeness *and* separateness.

Of course, to do this we need to be both self-aware, and self-responsible. We have to be able to compassionately witness the surges of feelings within us, and then name them. This also means being willing to pull back from the desire to blame our partners, or to try to get them to be different so as not to trigger us.

SCORE to the Rescue

When we can use the SCORE Process – step back into ourselves, connect to ourselves with compassion, observe the origin of our feelings, and remember our responsibility for our feelings (while relinquishing our sense of responsibility for our partners' feelings), we can handle PAP and PEP triggers more skillfully, without getting derailed by them.

Yes, these triggers, like other triggers, make us feel as if our lives are in danger. But no, they actually are not. We are two independent adults in a relationship based on mutuality – or at least, if we want happy, healthy intimacy, that needs to be our goal!

Some peoples' intimacy and autonomy styles are definitely more similar than those of other people. For instance, both Michelle and I are introverts who need a fair amount of time alone, so even if the exact amounts we need, and the exact moments we need it, are not identical, we can understand each other more easily than we might if one of us were a major extrovert.

But it's never possible to find a partner whose desires, preferences and needs always precisely mirror our own – so in any relationship, no matter how compatible the partners are, it's important to learn how to work with PAP and PEP through the SCORE process.

There are many other healing practices which can help us diminish both the intensity and the frequency of our PAP and PEP attacks. Inner child rescue, or soul retrieval, is a very powerful tool which has helped me a great deal, and which I've also used successfully with many clients. Working on the symbolic, energetic and somatic levels can help us heal much more deeply than mindfulness alone – though mindfulness is a very helpful first step.

But again, this healing can only take place when someone is willing to acknowledge and take responsibility for the fact that the origins of her PAP or PEP lie within her, rather than assigning responsibility to her partner.

If Only I Had Known...

How might my relationship with Emily played out differently if both of us had understood and been willing to work with, our PAP and our PEP?

First, we could have acknowledged that we each needed both closeness and separateness. Then we could have given ourselves and each other some compassion for the ways our needs were colliding in that vulnerable moment, so early in a new relationship.

Once we had done that, Emily might have been able to manage her PAP in a different way. If she had been able to work with her abandonment fears rather than trying to control me, it would have given me space to feel compassion for her, and to get out of PEP myself.

Of course, I could also say this in reverse. If I had been able to work more skillfully with my PEP, that would also have made it easier for Emily to get out of PAP! But either way, the key is for both people to take responsibility for their own feelings and work with them, rather than blaming or trying to change their partner.

Now, we're making all of this sound easy. And once you're well-practiced with the SCORE process, it actually can be. But it's also important to acknowledge that when we're first learning to work with all of this, it can feel *really* hard. That's because most of the brain actually shuts down when we get triggered, in an effort to help us fight or run from mortal danger. If you're actually *in* mortal danger, that can save your life. But when you're just arguing with your partner, that brain process makes it much harder to work things out.

The SCORE Process addresses that by helping you get *out* of the triggered state – the "amygdala hijack," which we describe in the chapter on SCORE – and back to your wiser self.

The good news is that the more you work to dismantle your triggers, the easier it gets – and over time, some of the triggers go away altogether. SCORE and the other processes we've described are the path to emotional freedom.

But another key is getting your mind on board. In other words, you need to stop *believing in* and *identifying with* the story of your emotions. The four Byron Katie questions we discussed in Roadmap Week 5 can help you with that, too.

Seth, a spiritual being channeled by Jane Roberts, had a very funny comment about this. "You don't confuse the bacon and eggs you ate this morning with 'yourself,'" he remarked, "So why do you think of your feelings as 'yourself'? Just like the bacon and eggs, they're simply passing through you."

Recognizing True Differences

Even though we all need both closeness and separateness, different people do prefer different expressions of these needs. For instance, some couples can live together happily in a one-room apartment; others need separate bedrooms, or at least some separate physical space; still others prefer not to live together at all. Some people navigate their fear of abandonment by insisting on monogamous relationships; knowing that their partner will be sexually faithful helps them feel safe. But other people may adopt the opposite strategy, since the fear of being abandoned by one lover can lessen if they know they have another lover, or two or three, on call.

We don't mean to suggest that PAP is the only reason why people might choose monogamy or polyamory; there are many other factors involved. But since many monogamous and some polyamorous people tend to point fingers at people in the other camp, we think it's helpful to observe that either choice might emerge as a response to the same basic fear.

Of course, it does make things easier to partner with someone whose preferences around closeness and distance are somewhat similar to your own. If you yearn to live together and share a bed, and your partner would rather live next door or maybe even across town, you'll have some negotiating to do. But if neither one of you is triggered, this kind of negotiation gets much easier. And over time, with mindfulness, compassion, trust and intimacy, both

PAP and PEP tend to fade – so our preferences can mellow, or even shift.

How We've Worked It Out

Michelle and I are experimenters, and we've tried on practically every housing configuration during our eight years together. We've lived apart; we've lived in separate units of a duplex; we've lived together in a group house; we've lived together in our own place and even shared a bedroom. At this point, we live together, but have separate bedrooms and study spaces. (I actually think my first choice would be to live in adjacent cottages, or on separate floors or in separate wings of a big house, but we haven't managed that yet.)

Having built-in separate space really supports us, not only in being separate, but also in connecting. When we want to cuddle or be sexual, we get to say "Your place or mine?" And even though we see each other all day, every day, the electricity still crackles between us when we actively choose to come closer together.

Since we're both homebodies who also work from home, having some form of built-in space from one another is especially important for us. If either or both of us worked an outside job every day, we might get enough daily separateness to make us want to share a bedroom.

There are many ways for couples to work out their needs for closeness and distance; there is no single formula that is right for all of us. Or rather, the formula that's right for everyone involves using a process like SCORE – and what you do after that, once you're empowered, is up to you.

CHAPTER 17

If Only I Had Known...
Disaster Story #2

Listening to Limerence: A Not-So-Happy Love Story

"No," Lou said, turning her face away from mine. "I can't go there."

We were lying in my bed, and I'd taken my shirt off and slid on top of her. I was still madly in lust with her, and I had hoped that the feel of my breasts against her would re-awaken some desire in Lou, too. But she remained stiff and unyielding. Frustrated and hurt, I put my shirt back on, left the room and cried.

Lou and I had known each other for only a few months, and for most of that time our relationship had been long distance. We'd met just two weeks before I was scheduled to move out of state for my first university teaching job. I had recently ended a long-term partnership with a woman who'd been chronically ill for most of our seven years together, and I felt starved for fun and sex. I was also excited and overwhelmed by my new freedom, and nervous about moving and beginning my new career. It was a dangerous combination.

The first time Lou and I really talked, our conversation was mostly flirting. The next day, I felt as if my body had been taken over by a sex-crazed alien. Going to bed with Lou was *all* I could think about. My lust had a will of its own, and masturbating did nothing to quell it; in fact, it seemed to fan the flames.

I now know that I had plunged headfirst into limerence.

Evidently Lou felt the same way, because she soon started instant-messaging me, and pretty soon we were having IM sex. (This was in the days before cell phones and texting.) Then, as quickly as we could manage it, we got between the sheets.

Hours later, as we lingered in post-sex bliss, Lou started opening up to me. She told me first about her difficult childhood as a boyish adopted baby-dyke in the Midwest, and then about her most recent girlfriend, who had broken her heart. For me, lust and tenderness is an even more potent combination than lust alone. I was hooked.

And yet I was about to move 2000 miles away.

What would *you* have done?

Here's what I did: I asked Lou if she wanted to move to Ohio with me. And she said Yes.

We Were in Limerence, Not Love

Deep intimacy is one of the most amazing feelings – perhaps *the* most amazing feeling – we get to experience in our human lives. And real intimacy between two separate, differentiated people who know, trust, appreciate, admire, respect and love one another is the most amazing of all.

But that's not where Lou and I were when we made our big decision. We barely knew each other. So, although we were head-over-heels in what we thought was love, we were actually just in the blissfully merged but unsustainable state psychologists call *limerence*.

Limerence feels like love, but it's not. It's actually a product of brain chemistry. When two people first get attracted to each other, the brain starts pumping out all sorts of endogenous opiates – your own natural equivalent of heroin – and you get "high on love."

But when you're in limerence, you can't see or think clearly. You're every bit as stoned as you would be if you'd drunk a bottle of whiskey or taken a large quantity of some feel-good drug.

We all know that "honeymoon state" when the new woman is all we can think and talk about, and we move through the world in a dreamy daze and/or a near-constant state of sexual arousal. It's fun. It's amazing. It feels great. And that's the state Lou and I were in as I packed my boxes, taking breaks for a quickie as frequently as possible. (She had some things to attend to in California, so we had agreed that she would move to join me several months later.)

Yes, limerence feels great. But the truth is, it feels pretty much the same no matter who you're in limerence with. Being in limerence is not the result of deeply seeing and knowing someone, and feeling deeply seen and known by her. It's just a way of being stoned.

So the truth is, I was "under the influence" when I invited Lou to move across the country with me – and thus became part of the great lesbian cliché ("What does a lesbian bring on the second date? A U-Haul.")

Couples of all sexual orientations experience limerence, but it's often particularly intense for lesbians and queer women – maybe because women tend to embrace it with more abandon than men do.

Yet limerence is destined to fade. It *has* to fade – it's simply not possible for our brains to keep on pumping out all those extra endorphins forever. Nor would it be psychologically healthy if they could.

In order to develop genuine intimacy and love, we need to leave that blissed-out, merged state behind. Just as we separated from our mothers as toddlers, we have to separate from our girl-friends. This doesn't necessarily mean we need to break up with them, of course. But we do need to somehow reclaim our sense of being a whole, separate human being as the limerence ends.

The Drama of Merging & Un-Merging

Unfortunately for Lou and me, we found ourselves plunged into the work of un-merging the moment she arrived in Ohio with all of her worldly possessions. Transitioning from the merged state back to experiencing ourselves as separate beings is necessary and healthy, but it can be a bumpy ride. And it was especially bumpy for us.

Lou was understandably freaked-out at having changed her entire life to move thousands of miles with/for someone she barely knew (though she couldn't articulate that at the time.) And *I* was freaked-out by realizing I'd made a huge commitment to a delight-fully fun, sexy woman, and now found myself cohabiting with a withdrawn, argumentative woman who wouldn't even let me touch her.

Merging is not the same as intimacy. In fact, the merged state *prevents* real intimacy. This is because adult intimacy can only take place between two separate, distinct beings. Although merging initially feels blissful, within a matter of weeks or months it will become confining and suffocating.

So the un-merging between Lou and me would have had to happen anyway – but if we hadn't thrown a cross-country move and vastly premature commitment into the mix, it might have been a more gentle process.

Instead, we went from blissful limerence into full-on individu-ation conflict – the same kind of conflict that makes two-year-olds "terrible" – in a matter of days. To make matters worse, we had no foundation of intimacy or trust to help us weather the storm. All we'd had was lust, and now that was gone, at least for Lou.

Looking back, I can see that Lou was actually responding to a healthy impulse by trying hard to re-establish a separate sense of self. But all I knew at the time was that she wouldn't let me near her. Then one day we had a huge, painful fight – and afterward ended up in bed, where we made love for the first time since Lou's arrival in Ohio. It was the first time I'd ever experienced the phenomenon known as "make-up sex."

The sex was great, but my heart still felt heavy from all our fighting. A few days later, the pattern repeated itself – after several hours of hostile, painful talking, somehow the edges between us blurred and we went to bed again.

It felt wonderful – and confusing – to experience so much joy touching and being touched by the same woman with whom I'd so recently been locked in conflict. And although I wanted the joy of that touching, I couldn't trust it. I loved having sex with Lou, but I didn't want us to have to keep fighting in order to get there.

Now I can understand that Lou was terrified of how merged she felt with me. After all, she'd given up her whole life in California and moved cross-country to be with me, a woman she barely knew. So in hindsight I can understand why she withdrew from me both emotionally and sexually.

At the time, though, it was very triggering to me. I'd just emerged from a long relationship in which I'd cared for an ill partner – and barely had sex – for years. The last thing I wanted was a difficult, sexless relationship with a brand-new live-in girlfriend.

So I kept pushing hard for reconnection, which meant Lou had to keep working hard to push me away. But big fights left her feeling safely separate – so then she felt safe enough to reach toward me again.

If Only I Had Known...

If Lou and I had actually had more of a foundation of genuine affection and trust, we would have been much better off. And if we'd also understood what was happening, and had the willingness and tools to deal with it, we might have made things work.

But the truth was, we had confused limerence with love. We'd attempted to form a partnership from a connection better suited for a two-week fling. And we'd also stirred up such an emotional mess with each other that it would have taken a lot of work to get us onto solid footing – work we had neither the skills, nor the commitment to each other to do.

Lou's and my relationship played out with extra intensity because of the move – but the same pattern plays out between many new lesbian and queer couples, even without a U-Haul. Most of us have experienced that rush of connection so strong that it just "feels right" with a brand-new lover – though over time, if we're wise, we learn to enjoy that feeling *and* respond with more caution at the same time.

In fact, about a decade after my misadventure with Lou, I found myself lying in an attic bedroom with Michelle, making blissful love. The same phrase kept coming to my mind over and over. It was so strong I had to force myself not to say it. The phrase was *I want to marry you.* Finally, I did say it, though I hedged a bit. (I didn't propose; I just told the truth. "The phrase 'I want to marry you' keeps coming into my mind.") She looked at me with shock and delight. "I was thinking the same thing." We had only known each other for ten weeks.

The connection between Michelle and me was real, and at this point, 9+ years later, we know that it withstood the test of time.

But neither of us could have known that then. It was just too soon. Fortunately, we knew that – so even though we acknowledged that impulse toward marriage then, we didn't act on it until eight years later.

How Could Lou and I Have Done Things Differently?

We could have chosen to get to know each other much better before making plans for Lou to move cross-country to be with me. Of course, since we were going to be living nearly 3000 miles apart, this would have been difficult – but not impossible. (The truth is, by the time two months had passed and Lou was beginning to pack up her things, I already had my doubts – but it felt "too late to back out.")

I could have listened to my instincts and backed out, or slowed things down, before Lou actually moved.

If I had slowed our relationship down, I believe I would have recognized that Lou and I were well-suited to have a brief, fun, hot affair – but *not* to be partners. If we had managed to just have that affair, without trying to take things further, our connection might still be a pleasant memory for us both – rather than a train wreck that makes me wince. (Lou and I aren't in contact, so I can't say for sure how she feels about the whole thing now – but I know it was at least as traumatic for her as it was for me.)

I think the biggest moral from Lou's and my sad story is: *Don't make big life and relationship decisions while you're in limerence.*

CHAPTER 18

If Only I Had Known...
Relationship Disaster Story #3

How I Processed Myself Right Into A Devastating Breakup

I couldn't sleep. I couldn't eat. I sat in the big green chair in my living room, feeling as if I would cry forever. I felt everything the pop songs said, and more. *You were my world. I'm lost without you. You were my everything.*

Late one night, I even called a suicide hotline. I wasn't actively thinking about killing myself, but I just couldn't imagine how to go on without Sarah. She was the first woman with whom I'd ever truly wanted "forever," and she had broken up with me suddenly and without explanation.

True, we'd been living thousands of miles apart for the past five months, but I'd flown out to visit her every few weeks – and occasionally she'd flown back to visit me too. True, we'd gone through some rough times on our visits, but we always seemed to patch things up by the end. We spoke on the phone, emailed or IMed every day. (This was in the days before texting.)

We were deeply in love – or so I'd thought.

Where had we gone wrong?

I flashed back in my mind to five months before, when Sarah and I had driven cross country together. Sarah, a chef, was moving to California for a special culinary program, and I'd convinced her to let me tag along for the ride. (We both lived in Ohio at the time.)

Actually, Sarah had been hesitant about having me come, but I had convinced her. I was madly in love with her, and we didn't get to spend nearly as much time together as I wanted – so the thought of having her all to myself for a long car trip sounded like heaven.

And for the first few days, it *was* heaven. I remember listening to Iron and Wine's soft acoustics on the stereo as I drove through the Nashville evening rain with Sarah asleep beside me. It was one of those moments of such piercing happiness that I could truly not imagine anything better.

Then there were the miles in Texas when Sarah was behind the wheel, but somehow still made love to me with one hand by putting just the right kinds of pressure on me through my jeans. It was definitely the most fun I've ever had on a highway.

How Things Began to Fall Apart

But further west in Texas, we stopped to spend Thanksgiving with Sarah's family, and when we got back on the road, Sarah was quiet – too quiet for my comfort. "What's wrong?" I asked. Getting little response, I tried again a little while later. "What are you thinking?" Still, Sarah didn't turn my way.

The miles wore on. Texas is a big, big state. And although Sarah was physically present beside me, it felt as if she wasn't there at all.

Her silence brought up panic in me. All I knew was that I needed contact from her, reassurance. I needed her to smile at me, hold my hand, reach out to me in some way. Perhaps if she had been able to say, "I love you, but I just need a few hours to be with my own thoughts right now," I could have managed.

But she didn't say that, and I didn't stop pushing. When we stopped for gas, I tried to kiss her. She turned her face away.

After that, I cried for hours, silently, in the seat beside her, as she drove and drove.

Eventually we stopped for the night at a tacky little cabin-style motel. Sarah quickly lay down on the bed and started reading. The only way I could think to comfort myself was to take a bath, so I began running the water. The hot water ran out when the tub was just one-third full. I closed the bathroom door, sat on the cold tile floor, and sobbed.

Then I got mad. How could Sarah do this to me? I deserved better.

I dried my face, swung open the bathroom door, and confronted her.

I honestly can't remember what happened next. I guess I've blocked it out. I do know that we remained bruised and distant from each other for the whole rest of the several-day drive.

By the time we got to California we had patched up our connection a little, but were still guarded and wary with one another. I could tell Sarah was trying, but neither of us knew how to make our way back from the pain of the abyss.

I spent three or four days with Sarah in California, helping her look for a place to live, before I was scheduled to fly home. On our way to the airport, we stopped for some Mexican food. As we sat there in the tacqueria, ranchera music blaring from the speakers, I looked at the face of the woman I loved. Then I put some salsa on my rice, scooped it up with a piece of corn tortilla, and calculated my words.

I knew that what I was about to say would hurt Sarah. I ran my tongue over the place inside me that wanted to hurt her. And then I said it.

"You know, I'll never forgive you for what you did to me on our trip here. Our relationship will never be the same."

I didn't realize that I was, in that very moment, ensuring that my hurtful statement would become the truth. Our relationship *would* never be the same again – but I was at least as responsible for that as Sarah.

Of course, we both cried. I was still crying an hour later when I got on the plane. Over the next few months we sent hundreds of emails back and forth, and spent many long hours on the phone.

I flew to see her in January; she visited me in February; I went back to California in March. In fact, we had a wonderful time on that visit, or so I thought. There was our trip down the coast to Malibu, and that passionate interlude in the kitchen, when I was wearing the peach-colored silk slip she liked so much…

Yet, just two weeks later, by phone, she broke up with me.

Where had we gone wrong?

If I'd Known Then What I Know Now...

It took me many years to really understand what had gone wrong between Sarah and me – or, even more specifically, where *I* had gone wrong. By then, I'd gone through two more painful breakups and begun yet another relationship. And, finally, that relationship – my relationship with Michelle – was different. But it was largely because I myself had changed.

I've always been a strong-willed woman , though my self-confidence masks a part of me that is tender, vulnerable and scared. Still, the mask can be intimidating. Sarah used to call it my "debate team personality." Another girlfriend, Jana, called it the "lawyer" in me.

And that debate team personality or lawyer-like self was very good at trying to convince my partners that I was right – and therefore, that they were wrong – in any dispute we had.

I did this a lot with Sarah.

I'm femme in appearance, but have a strong personality, and – perhaps because "opposites attract" – I have tended to pick partners who are softer and gentler than me, even though they look more butch. Sarah fit that pattern. She was truly no match for me in an argument. At the time, I didn't realize just how big a problem that was.

By Blaming Sarah for My Feelings, I Pushed Her Away

When Sarah and I were together, I did a lot of "processing." Now I can see that that led to the downfall of our relationship.

The problem with "processing" is that it's usually a way women communicate about our feelings *without taking full responsibility for them.*

When you don't take full responsibility for your own feelings, it means you blame the other person for them. And that's what I did – and what people who "process" usually do – without even realizing it.

The problem is that when you're blaming someone else for your feelings, or trying to get her to change her behavior so that you'll stop feeling what you're feeling, "communicating your feelings" can turn into a subtle attack. And attacking a partner will *always* damage a relationship.

Let's compare two different approaches – processing and SCORE – in relation to the same situation: the way Sarah withdrew from me on our cross country trip. Below, I'll imagine that Sarah and I are talking a few weeks after the trip, when we've each had some time to think things through. This will give you a clear illustration of how different processing really is from the SCORE Process.

Processing Example (Not recommended.)

"Sarah, I want you to know that it really hurt me when you stopped talking to me on our trip. It pushed my buttons and brought up all my fears, and I'm still having trouble accepting the fact that you did that to me.

And it's especially unfair given that I had taken all that time to make the cross-country drive with you. I know you were probably doing the best you could, but I just feel unsafe with you now.

I don't know how I can trust someone who just stops communicating with me like that. Communication is really important to me, and so is physical affection, and you withdrew both of those from me. And it was at a very vulnerable time for me, since I was sitting beside you in the car for all those miles, and there was no way for me to get away. That's why it was so damaging..."

This example is probably pretty close to what I actually said to Sarah. And at first glance, many of these statements may seem reasonable. After all, I'm using quite a few "I-statements," which is what therapists generally recommend.

Statements like "It pushed my buttons and brought up all my fears" even make it seem, for an instant, as if perhaps I'm going to own the fact that I got triggered – but then I go on to say *"And I'm having trouble accepting that you did this to me."* That language – "you did this to me" – is a giveaway, making it clear that I am blaming Sarah for what happened, rather than acknowledging my own responsibility for my emotions, and for co-creating our interaction.

Again, processing can sometimes pose as self-responsible com-munication. In this example, I say a lot of things that seem like they sprang from the pages of a book about healthy communica-tion – phrases like "I feel unsafe," "I don't know how I can trust," "Communication and physical affection are important to me."

But if you read more closely, you'll notice that despite giving lip service to Sarah's experience by saying "I know you were prob-ably doing the best you could," what I am actually doing in this monologue is haranguing Sarah, blaming her for my feelings, and resisting taking any responsibility for my own experience.

(Oh yes, and I was even trying to make her feel bad for the time I took off to make the trip with her – after I was the one who talked her into letting me come along!)

My point here is not that this kind of processing is "bad," or that women are wrong to do it. I was doing the best I knew how to do at the time, and if you've ever "processed" in this way, you probably were too.

The problem is this: *Processing damages our relationships.* It doesn't work. It doesn't get our partners to stop triggering us. And it doesn't help us create the happy, healthy relationships we actu-ally want.

In the processing example, even though I'm using psycholog-ical language, *I am still telling Sarah that I was right and she was wrong.* Even if she doesn't realize in the moment why she feels so bad, it will register on some level, and will inevitably erode our connection.

Let's imagine about how Sarah might have responded to my processing. There are really only a few possible ways.

- She might have defended herself against my attacks.
- She might have attacked me back.

- Or, she might have "knuckled under," agreed that I was right and she was wrong, and begged for my forgiveness.

Obviously, becoming defensive and/or attacking back doesn't lead to a loving interaction or create more intimacy. Yet most of us find it hard to avoid one of those two responses when we feel attacked.

A very conciliatory or conflict-avoidant person might manage the third option: she might avoid overtly defending herself or attacking me, take responsibility for everything I accused her of, and promise to change.

But even if she did that on the outside, on the inside she'd be amassing resentment, losing trust, and hardening herself against me.

(I've conferred with Michelle – who *is* a very conciliatory person – about this, so I've gotten it from the horse's mouth here. Michelle says that in her own long-term relationship with a girlfriend who processed a lot, she never attacked back, and rarely defended herself. She always just apologized. But over time, that killed her natural generosity, love, trust and feeling of connection to her partner.)

So, even if I had appeared to "win" in the short term and wrestled a "mea culpa" out of Sarah, *nobody actually wins with processing*. Communication without self-responsibility destroys relationships.

Now let's look at what I might have said to Sarah if I had been able to SCORE, using the SCORE process described earlier in this book.

SCORE Example (Recommended.)

"Sarah, I've been wanting to talk about what happened on our trip, because I know it was really hard, scary and painful for both of us.

I've thought about it a lot, and I've realized that the reason I reacted so strongly when you withdrew was that it brought up some really primal abandonment fears for me. For some reason, having someone be physically present but emotionally absent is just about the most terrifying thing for me.

I wish I'd had better ways to cope with that terror, but I just got completely overtaken by it. I feel really badly that I pushed so hard for more contact, rather than just being able to accept that you had to go be inside yourself for a while.

I know things might have played out really differently if I had just known how to take better care of myself, rather than trying to demand something from you that you weren't capable of giving in that moment.

I wish I had just been able to tell you how scared I felt, without making you wrong in the process. And, I'm especially sorry that I said that hurtful thing to you in the taco place, about our relationship never being the same again.

The truth is, I knew even before I said those words that they would hurt you. In fact, in that moment there was a part of me that wanted to hurt you, as a way of getting revenge for how much I felt you had hurt me. I really regret that.

Although what happened on our trip was really painful for me, I know you weren't deliberately trying to hurt me, and you certainly didn't deserve for me to deliberately hurt you."

Can you see the difference? This SCORE example is brimming with self-responsibility. I'm still telling Sarah about my feelings – in fact, I'm telling her about even more feelings than I did in the processing example. I've named my abandonment fear, my regret at having pushed her, my wish that I could have told her how scared I felt, and my sadness at having been deliberately hurtful to her. I've also acknowledged how painful our trip was for me.

But I've named all of these feelings *without any undertone of blaming or attacking Sarah*. I'm acknowledging my own responsibility, and my triggers. I'm admitting that there was a moment in which I actually wanted to hurt her, and apologizing for it. I'm letting her know that I wish I'd had better skills for taking care of myself. And I'm making it clear that I know that this whole issue has been hard, scary and painful for her, just as it has been for me.

If I had been able to speak to Sarah with this degree of self-responsibility, it would have opened up space for an entirely different set of possible responses – all of which could have helped us to *build intimacy* even during the course of this difficult conversation.

How might Sarah have responded?

- She might have felt moved by my vulnerability, and responded with tenderness.

- She might have felt relieved that I wasn't attacking her – which then could have allowed her to feel more open to me.

- Because I was acknowledging my mistakes and regrets, she might have been able to acknowledge that she had made mistakes or had regrets, too. For instance, after hearing my apologies, she might have found herself able to say, "You know, I wish I'd been able to handle things differently, too. I wish I'd been able to actually tell you that I just needed some space. I'm sorry I couldn't. I realize it was really scary for you."

- My acknowledgement that I had actually *wanted* to hurt her – but that I regretted that – might have helped her relax and feel safer around me again.

All of these positive, intimacy-restoring reactions could really only have come about in relation to my using the SCORE process. Processing just doesn't get us there.

If you read both examples – Processing and SCORE – again, and actually let yourself notice how each feels in your body, I believe you'll viscerally experience why that is so. Being "processed at" shuts us down. Being part of a SCORE conversation opens us up.

It's impossible for me to know exactly how Sarah would have responded if I had been able to SCORE. But I *can* say that before I learned to SCORE, my relationships were painful, and since I learned to SCORE, I've had a wonderful, deep, rich, sweet, passionate and stable connection.

And since Michelle has the same kind of soft, sweet personality Sarah had – and tends to blame herself or withdraw rather than fight, just as Sarah did – I can also see that if I hadn't learned to SCORE, I would have hurt Michelle as much as I hurt Sarah. I am so grateful I don't have to do that any more.

I'm sorry, Sarah. I wish I had known then what I know now.

CHAPTER 19

As I Was Learning What I Know Now: Relationship Semi-Disaster #4

Feelings Aren't Fatal (Though They Can Feel That Way.)

"I'm sorry," Jana told me on the phone. "I'm going to be late."

"*How* late?" I asked her, my voice tight.

Jana and I didn't get much time together. Her schedule and other commitments only allowed her to see me once a week, and even then, she could never spend the night. But on this particular evening, she'd had the day off from work, and I'd initially hoped we could spend more time together – so I wasn't very happy about it when she told me she'd agreed to help some friends paint their house.

"Not very happy" was actually an understatement. I was angry. I felt cheated, neglected, deprived, unvalued, taken for granted, and wronged – and even though I didn't say those things directly, I made sure Jana knew I was displeased.

She had agreed to be at my house at 6:00 p.m. Now, she sounded reluctant to say just how late she'd be. "Um, maybe 7:00?" But shortly before 7:00, she called again to say it would be "more like 7:30 or 8:00." At 8:00, she called again to tell me she'd be even later.

As it turned out, Jana didn't get to my house until 9:30 that night. But on this particular night, I finally did something right. I'd been taking a course that taught me how to take responsibility for my own feelings. I'd been working with a therapist who encouraged the same thing. And I hadn't been the fastest learner in the world, but something was finally sinking in.

So, from 8:00 until 9:00, between Jana's calls, I lay on my couch and let myself feel my own feelings – befriended them and let them move through me, without getting attached to the mental "stories" that had piggybacked on top of them – in a way I'd never fully done before.

As I've said, I was very good at making cases for why I was right, and my partner was wrong. In this instance, that wasn't hard to do. Jana was being inconsiderate, and part of me felt I had a right to be angry or hurt.

But on this particular night, I also recognized that the crushed, outraged panic I felt was all too familiar. I had felt it before, with other partners, and if my relationship with Jana ended, I was certain I'd feel it again.

In that moment, I felt as if my heart simply couldn't take many more breakups. So instead of breaking up, I knew I had to break *through*.

So I lay on the couch, pulled a blanket over my head, and let myself shake and cry. I did my best to stop replaying my "story" in my head – the story about why I was right and Jana was wrong – and to simply feel my feelings and let them pass through my body instead.

It was one of the hardest and most important things I've ever done.

By the time Jana got to my house that night, I was genuinely calm. Not faking it, not stuffing it, but calm. I had entered some new country within myself, and planted a flag.

Without knowing it, I had used the SCORE process for the very first time.

Ultimately, my relationship with Jana didn't survive – but it didn't matter. The truth was, we weren't all that compatible outside the bedroom, anyway. Our breakup was still hellish, but afterward, I felt a new resolve.

It took three more years for me to meet Michelle and create a truly healthy, happy relationship. But during that time, I kept using the SCORE process – by which I mean, I kept examining my own triggers, the feelings that had repeatedly caused me problems in my relationships.

I connected to myself with compassion; I explored the origin of those feelings, and I took responsibility for them. They hadn't been caused by my partners. They belonged to *me*.

That movement into self-responsibility was phenomenally freeing and empowering. Once I owned my own feelings, really accepted them as mine, I could work with them in healing ways, rather than pouring energy into futile attempts to make other people be different.

The truth is, no matter how vehemently I argued or how articulately I stated my case, I had never really been able to change my girlfriends. (And I'd bet you've never really been able to change yours, either.)

What I finally realized, that fateful night with Jana, was that it *was* within my power to change my own emotional experience. I didn't have to be at the mercy of the sticky amalgam of past and present pain which had led me to lash out, punish and attempt to control my partners. I could actually dissolve those hard knots of hurt inside me, and bring a more mature, gentle, self-responsible presence to my relationships.

I Had Chosen Jana On Purpose

The interesting thing is that Jana had been up-front with me from the beginning. She had a long-term partner, but sex had died out between them, so she'd gotten her partner's okay to seek another lover – and I had signed on to be that lover. So I knew from the beginning that we would only be able to see each other once a week.

In other words, I had agreed up-front to a situation guaranteed to push my abandonment buttons! I was only half-conscious of it at the time, but it was certainly a perfect set-up for me to work on those buttons, and make progress in dismantling those triggers.

Of course this wasn't the kind of relationship I would want over the long haul. But having experienced feeling smothered and suffocated in other relationships, I had PEP as well as PAP – so the same unavailability that set off my PAP was a great reassurance to my PEP

The internal work I did while I was with Jana – and, equally, the years I spent being single after our relationship ended – had a huge impact on my being able to become a more emotionally mature, self-responsible partner. And that, in turn, led me to attract Michelle, who'd been doing her own work to become emotionally mature and self-responsible before we met.

Michelle was and is everything I could have hoped for in a partner: wise, vulnerable, spiritual, kind, self-aware, brilliant, compassionate, dedicated to growth – and cute, too. Naturally, she also brought with her some issues and wounds which pushed my buttons. We had some work to do. But now, finally, I had – and still have – a way to do it.

Michelle and I are very well-matched. We love and trust each other deeply; we laugh a lot, and we have a great time together. But we're also aware that if we had met ten years earlier, we would have been disastrous for each other. If I hadn't taught myself to SCORE, the patterns I played out with Lou, Sarah, Emily, Jana and others would undoubtedly have sunk my union with Michelle as well.

Who Do You Blame?

Each of us has a default pattern around blame. When conflict arises, some of us tend to blame ourselves – we think, "This is my fault. I'm bad, I'm wrong, I'm broken, I'm unlovable."

Some of us have the opposite pattern. When we feel bad, we tend to blame other people. "What *I* want is perfectly reasonable, so why won't you give it to me?"

As I've described, I'm in the latter category. So when my partners triggered difficult feelings in me, my immediate response was always to *blame them* – to see them as wrong for having hurt me or let me down (and then to try to convince them that how I see it is actually how it is.)

Michelle, on the other hand, does the opposite. She's gender-queer to my femme-of-center; she's tall to my short; she's yin to my yang... and she's also self-blame to my blame. In other words, instead of blaming me when things go wrong, she immediately blames herself.

So you can see how this would play out, if we didn't know how to SCORE. I'd blame her, and she'd blame herself. We'd both be pointing the finger... at Michelle. Over time, she'd feel worse and worse about herself – but underground, her resentment toward me would grow, and her sense of love and trust would fade.

I know the pattern well, because that's what happened with Jana and Sarah. On the other hand, Emily and Lou blamed *me* – so I know how that one feels, too. Neither of those positions, blaming or being blamed, is any fun. And both make a happy, healthy relationship impossible.

Who's Right? Who's Wrong? Who's Better? Who's Worse?

Oops. Wrong questions.

There's nothing better – or worse – about tending to blame others, or blame oneself. Each perspective is skewed; each holds one part of the truth, and ignores others.

It's like the parable of the blind men and the elephant. The guy who touches the elephant's tusk and says "An elephant is like a spear" isn't wrong, but neither is the guy who tugs on the elephant's tail and says "No, no, an elephant is like a rope." The whole elephant of any human interaction is almost always bigger than we can see in any given moment.

Yet even when we know all of that, these default patterns – blaming others or blaming ourselves – seem to be pretty firmly set in our personality structures. I'm a big believer in healing and change, so I would never say these patterns *can't* change. But in this case, I've found it's faster and more effective to just "add consciousness and stir" (if you're baking a cake of happiness and harmony, that is.)

So, when I get into a conflict with Michelle, I "add consciousness" by deliberately reminding myself that I tend to blame others rather than take self-responsibility, and I work hard to ask myself: *How might I be doing that here? What more do I need to see about my own role in whatever is happening?*

And, as you'll see in a moment, that line of questioning leads me right into the SCORE process.

As I've said, if Michelle and I couldn't SCORE – if we didn't have what we call "Conscious Girlfriend" skills – all our conflicts would play out the same way: I would blame her, and she would blame herself. I would get angry, and she would get apologetic. I would tell her what I wanted her to do differently, and she would try to do it.

And pretty soon our love, trust and connection would be gone.

The SCORE Process – and the self-compassion, self-inquiry and self-responsibility that underlie it – are what enable our relationship to stay happy, healthy, intimate and strong.

So I'm very grateful for the pain that pushed me into learning to SCORE.

Thank you, Jana, for being so late that night.

CHAPTER 20

How Self-Love Changes Everything: Jeanette's Story

Like most of the women we work with, Jeanette, 49, deeply wanted emotionally intimate love. Here are some of the statements she wrote in response to our question, "What would that feel like to you?"

"I can be there with all the parts of myself, with no part left out. I'm able to show my feelings. I can be vulnerable, and so can my partner. It's free flowing, easy, natural, spontaneous, affectionate. I feel loved for who I am. My partner's not trying to change me. I can ask for what I want, and I can say when something's not OK with me."

Jeanette wanted love that could hold and accept each part of her – love in which she could finally allow herself to feel what she felt. Love in which she could stop trying to control herself, or control someone else. Love in which she could say Yes when she wanted to, and then let herself fully receive what someone else had to give – and love in which she could also say No when she needed to, and feel at ease with saying it.

When we asked Jeanette to imagine having this kind of love, she responded, *"I feel a warm feeling in my chest and stomach when I think about her. I accept her and appreciate her as she is, and feel the same from her. It feels unforced. Neither of us is controlling or being controlled. There's a sense of deep safety, trust, authenticity."*

What a beautiful, inspiring vision! Yet it was also painful for Jeanette to even think about this kind of love, because it was so different from anything she had ever experienced.

As we told Jeanette, "You can't find this kind of love no matter how hard you look for it."

That's because it's not something you can *find*. It's something you can only learn to *create* – both within yourself, and between you and another person.

Here's the mistake most of us make, and the mistake Jeanette had made – the pattern she had played out, over and over again.

The Drama of Love Between People Who Don't Love Themselves

Here's what usually happens.

You feel lonely, empty, disconnected. You know you're supposed to "love yourself," but you have no idea how to do that; it seems like a vague, meaningless concept, or an impossible goal. So you go looking for someone else to love you instead.

Sometimes she shows up quickly. Other times, it takes months or years of searching before you find that elusive "click." But then... here she is!

You enjoy each other's company. You've got things in common. There's laughter, long looks, electricity between you. There's a sweet, searching – or hot, passionate – first kiss.

Pretty soon you're in bed together every chance you get. It feels amazing. You just can't believe how perfect she is, how right it all feels. You start thinking, maybe even talking, about a future together. Perhaps on the strength of this feeling, the wonderful high of having found each other, you move in together. Maybe you even get married. Things are great.

Until they're not.

Chances are, whoever you found isn't deeply emotionally intimate with herself, either. At first, that doesn't seem like a problem. It's easy for you to see how wonderful she is, and you tell her that over and over. And she does the same with you. It's great.

Now all that stuff you might have heard about "needing to be able to love yourself before you can love someone else" seems like a myth. You're getting love. You're giving love. You've proven the pundits and naysayers wrong. Right?

Except…

Over time, it fades. Perhaps the end is slow, a gradual dimming of passion. Perhaps it all comes crashing down, suddenly and dramatically. Either way, you're left wondering: *What happened to our love? Where did it go? And will it ever be possible to get it back?*

Maybe you start to notice things about her that really bug you. You criticize her, or tell her how she should change, and she gets defensive.

Maybe she criticizes you, too, striking at sore spots she had previously seemed to love, or at least accept. Over time, more and more topics turn into danger zones – conversations you'd better stay away from. Your sense of safety and trust begins to slip away.

Maybe you start wanting more from her – more time, more affection, more sex, more closeness – and she pulls away. Or she wants more from *you*, and you feel crowded, suffocated.

Maybe you just stop talking. She works more, or spends more time on things that take her away from you. Or perhaps you're the one who does that. Either way, when you *are* together, it starts feeling kind of empty.

Maybe there's bickering. Not huge fights, just snappy exchanges that leave you a bit wary. You begin to talk more with your friends than with her. You talk to your friends *about* her, complaining or trying to figure out what's wrong.

Or maybe there *are* big fights. Huge blow-ups, where you yell, slam doors, cry for hours afterward. Or endless "processing sessions" where each of you tries to get the other one to hear you, to change.

Maybe you struggle through this for months or years before one or both of you calls it quits. Maybe you call it quits directly, by telling her you need to leave – or maybe you do it indirectly, or she does, by having an affair, or falling in love with someone else.

Then it takes more months or years to disentangle yourselves. There's so much you have to separate out – friends, belongings, money, memories. Sometimes there are even children, complicated custody arrangements and finances.

You walk around with a hole in your heart. There's bitterness, anger, hurt, grief. You feel betrayed – by her, or maybe by life. Underneath it all, there's a deep, agonizing confusion. *Where did we go wrong? What happened to our love?*

But chances are you never figure it out, so you stop trying. Instead, you get cynical about love – until you eventually meet someone else, and the whole cycle starts up again.

Limerence Isn't Love

As we've discussed elsewhere, limerence is the real cause of that initial "honeymoon stage" we often think is love. Limerence is a brain chemistry state that gets triggered when two people get attracted to each other. In limerence, you brain – and hers – pump out feel-good chemicals that make you see each other through rose-colored glasses.

When you're in limerence, you're literally high – stoned on brain chemicals, endogenous opiates that make you feel fantastic. But it's hard to develop real love while you're in limerence – both because most of us don't know how, and also because limerence makes it feel unnecessary. *We feel like we're already there. But we're not.*

Limerence does a great job of mimicking love – because in limerence, we feel safe, connected, cared-for and adored. In response, our best selves emerge. We get more tender, more generous, more open-hearted. This creates a positive momentum – the better we feel, the better we make our partners feel. The better our partners feel, the better they make *us* feel.

It's wonderful. It's beautiful. It's thrilling. It's amazing. But it doesn't last.

Although the exact duration of limerence is different for each person, in most cases it lasts less than a year. And when your brain chemistry returns to normal, the person you were so madly in love with looks imperfect again (which, of course, she is.)

And guess what? You look that way to her, too.

When that limerence high wears off, you need to know how to build real love and intimacy in its place. If you don't, you'll believe you've "fallen out of love," and go looking for someone else with whom you can "fall" all over again.

If neither of you knows how to love yourselves, you're likely to demand constant doses of reassurance from one another. But over time, demand will outpace supply. It's simply not sustainable to love someone else more or better than she can love herself – nor can she fill the hole in your soul that comes from your own lack of self-love.

Over time, since neither of you is getting what you need, negative patterns surface – criticism and blame, withdrawal, power struggles, bickering, fights, endless processing, affairs. This finishes the job, eroding the love you thought you shared.

How "Love" Turns to "Hate"

Have you ever wondered why two people who thought they loved each other deeply can later start hating each other?

The truth is, if "love" can turn to hate, it was never really love at all. Much of what we call love is actually dependence. The unspoken agreement is: *I can't feed myself, so I need you to feed me. As long as you feed me as much as I want, I feel "love" for you. But as soon as you can't, I don't.*

This is not the deeply fulfilling, lasting love we long for. It's a poor substitute, like flavored cardboard masquerading as nutritious food.

If you've grown cynical about love, if you've stopped believing in it, it's probably because you've gotten – and given – cardboard love instead of the real thing.

And if that's the case, it's not your fault. Chances are no one ever taught you how to build lasting love and intimacy. Even if your parents had a relatively good marriage, they probably didn't have the level of intimacy most lesbians want and expect from our relationships now.

Of course, many of our parents didn't have good relationships at all, so most of us grew up without any models for mature, sustainable love.

The capacity for real love lives within each of us, the way each seed holds the potential to become a plant. But because we don't know how to unlock that potential, most of us spend years or even decades trying to get love from another person, *even though we don't know how to give it.* Worse, we usually don't know how to receive it, either.

Buddhist folk tales tell about "hungry ghosts," beings who are constantly suffering because they are always famished. They have huge stomachs, but tiny little mouths and stick-thin throats. They suffer endlessly, because they simply can't take in the quantity of nourishment they need.

As soon as I heard about hungry ghosts, the image haunted me – because I recognized myself in it. *I was a hungry ghost in love* – or what I thought was love.

And chances are you are, too.

There's no shame in being a hungry ghost – but there's a lot of pain. (Well, actually there *is* shame, because we often feel deeply ashamed of needing love so badly, and also of our failure to find it. But there is nothing shameful about our need for love. It's just that we can't get it met until we learn how to love ourselves.)

The good thing is, "hungry ghosthood" is not a permanent condition. You can change it. You can learn to give yourself real self-compassion and love, and also to create that kind of connection with someone else in a way that will actually last.

Self-Love: The Foundation of The Relationship You Want

Many people say, "You can't love anyone else until you can love yourself." But we haven't actually found that to be true. Many people who don't love themselves *do* manage to love other people. But they're usually not very good at receiving love, or at creating healthy, joyful, emotionally connected relationships. That's because that kind of relationship can only be built upon a foundation of self-love.

Why do so many people today struggle with an absence of self-love? Self-hatred has reached epidemic proportions in contemporary Western culture. Although many psychologists and spiritual leaders have theories about why this may be so, no one knows for sure. However, it seems likely that lack of self-love emerges from misconceptions formed very early in our lives.

Jeanette's Path to Self-Love and Love

When Jeanette was born, her mother was depressed and overwhelmed. Jeanette's father was in the military overseas, and her mother was struggling to take care of the 3-year-old twins she already had.

To make matters worse, both of Jeanette's parents had hoped she would be a boy. Since she wasn't, they were relieved that at least she was a "good baby." Jeanette rarely cried, even when left alone for many hours. Since the twins needed so much attention, Jeanette's mother only paid attention to Jeanette at feeding time.

At 49, when she came to us for coaching, Jeanette struggled with her weight and with a persistent sense that she didn't deserve the things she wanted, like a great relationship, a promotion, and a bigger apartment. She had a deep conviction that she was unlovable, somehow "flawed at the core."

Although she didn't realize it at first, Jeanette's self-rejection emerged from the sense that she was a burden. Even in infancy, she had done her best to want and need as little as possible.

However, as she worked with the Metta practice and other self-love and self-compassion tools, Jeanette realized that her mother's feelings and behavior had actually *had nothing to do with her.* There wasn't anything wrong with *her;* any infant born into that household at that moment would have been a burden to a woman caring for 3-year-old twins on her own.

Jeanette had internalized her mother's stress – and her mother's disappointment at not having had a son – and took them to mean that there was something wrong, unlovable, flawed, about her. But

Metta and the visualizations we gave her helped her dislodge this ancient belief.

The truth is, it's easier than you think to start loving yourself. Recent research on the brain has shown us just how retrainable it is. Due to our *neuroplasticity*, it is entirely possible to create new neural pathways when we repeat a new habit, belief or thought often enough. But since repetition is the key, becoming able to love yourself does – like most other life changes – require a decision, a commitment.

Jeanette was ready. Although she worked with us for just 12 weeks, she did her homework between sessions, and took on the project of giving herself love and compassion with vigor.

And within a few weeks, she felt shifts. "Strangers on the street are smiling at me more," she reported to us with wonder. "My co-workers are more considerate of me. Healthier people are showing up in my life."

Then Thanksgiving came, and Jeanette went to visit her family. The visit wasn't easy, but it gave her some valuable opportunities to stand up for herself. Amazingly enough, at the end of the visit, Jeanette's mother apologized to her for not having been a better parent when Jeanette was small.

"I couldn't believe she said that," Jeanette said. "But somehow I know she wouldn't have, if not for the work I've been doing."

Three months after she began working with us, Jeanette gave notice on her apartment, and then found a place she liked better. She mentioned to her boss that she was moving, and her boss offered her a promotion to help pay her increased rent.

Big things had shifted. But the next item on the agenda was emotionally healthy love, and Jeanette was understandably scared to risk that one. She decided to take a break from working with us, and continue working with Metta and the other self-love practices we'd given her so she could keep getting stronger on her own.

Six months later, Jeanette contacted us again. She had met a woman she liked a lot, and though it was still early, she was already finding herself able to be honest, open and present in ways she had never been before. Even though they'd only been dating for a few weeks, she asked if she could have Natalie join her for some coaching sessions.

We worked with Jeanette and Natalie together for a month, and helped them both learn to speak even more openly to one another. It was truly beautiful to witness Jeanette's blossoming. Although Natalie was a quieter person, she had a deeply receptive quality – and a willingness to be emotionally honest – that we believed boded well for the couple.

Now, as we write these words, Jeanette and Natalie have been together for nine months, and in Jeanette's words, "Our relationship gets deeper each day. We're still taking it slow – we wouldn't even consider moving in together for at least another year. But we're really starting to share ourselves with each other. I would never have believed this was possible. I'm so grateful."

"You're the one who did the work." we reminded her.

CHAPTER 21

Jill's Story:
Making Peace With The Past

Jill was definitely the marrying kind. At 58, she'd had three long relationships with women. The first had ended amicably, when both she and her partner were in their twenties. But Jill had more pain about the ending of her second two relationships. Her second partner, Carrie, had had an affair while Jill was working out of town. And her third partner, Helen – with whom she'd spent 18 years and co-parented a child – had relapsed so many times into alcoholism that Jill knew she had to leave.

After her breakup with Helen, Jill spent five years single, until their son was out of the house. Then she had a brief relationship with a woman she'd met through work, who gave her a lot of mixed messages and turned out to be emotionally unavailable. Jill felt confused and hurt.

At that point, Jill found out about us, and signed up for coaching. She knew she wanted to find a new partner, but she had no idea how to enter "the dating scene." She felt too old, too out-of-practice, and too vulnerable.

It soon became clear that the first order of business was to help Jill make peace with her previous breakups. Her second partnership had ended when she was 35, and she had learned a lot since then, so she was pretty sure she wouldn't make the same mistakes again. But she still had some old hurt and confusion that she had never fully let herself feel. Away on a skiing weekend, she let the wind hit her hard, and yelled her pain into it – and afterward, she reported that she felt better.

The loss of Jill's long-term partner and co-parent was a bigger and fresher wound. Jill spent several sessions grieving in a way she hadn't allowed herself to do before. She also realized she had blamed herself for not having been able to save her partner, so we helped her do some self-forgiveness work.

Next, Jill needed help learning how to prioritize her own needs in a relationship. She was a classic caretaker, and tended to "adjust" to whatever her partners wanted and needed from her. But we felt – and Jill agreed – that at 58, it was time for that to change.

We helped Jill identify her most important priorities for her next relationship, and then work on believing that she deserved, and could have, a relationship which met those needs.

For instance, Jill had worked hard all of her adult life, and had saved a little nest-egg for herself. She wanted a partner who was similarly financially situated, or at least financially solid. "I don't want to be someone's Sugar Mama," she said bluntly.

Jill also loved skiing, and wanted to find a partner who didn't mind if Jill took skiing trips on her own, or with friends, for several weeks at a time. (This had been a big point of contention in her last relationship.)

And Jill was very physically active, so she really wanted a partner with whom she could share the activities she loved most.

We told Jill these were very reasonable "must-haves." And, not surprisingly, substance abuse was #1 on Jill's list of deal-breakers.

Jill was a great flirt, but she wasn't always good at being direct. So when she met Cherie on a hike and felt drawn to her, we coached her, date by date, on how to bring up the issues that mattered to her.

A month in, things were going pretty well between Jill and Cherie, but there had been a few glitches. Cherie often texted Jill during the day, but Jill didn't always have time to respond at length, which led to some miscommunications.

Jill was a little nervous to tell Cherie she'd been working with us ("Will she think that means there's something wrong with me?" she asked), but eventually she spilled the beans. We encouraged her to invite Cherie to join her for some coaching sessions – and Cherie was thrilled.

When we met with both women together, we could see how well-matched they were, but we also saw they needed some help with communicating. Jill had trouble asking directly for what she wanted, and Cherie was quick to make assumptions rather than get clarification.

So, we gave them some homework to do, identified patterns to watch out for, and cheered them on as they tried out new ways of communicating.

Jill and Cherie were also very nervous about when to begin having sex. They had very strong sexual chemistry and energy, but they were afraid of being taken over by it, so they had barely let themselves touch.

In a coaching session, they gradually become willing to open up about their fears. Although it took Jill a long time to get the words out, it turned out she was afraid that if sex wasn't perfect the first time, Cherie would lose interest.

Cherie laughed. "That won't happen," she reassured Jill. "I know it will take some time for us to get to know each other's bodies and feel comfortable. I'm totally okay with that process."

Jill felt more comfortable once she heard Cherie's words. But Cherie had heard us talk about limerence so many times that she was afraid maybe she and Jill shouldn't have sex until they were 100% sure they wanted to be together. We helped her realize that that probably wasn't realistic. It was okay for sex to become part of their process of getting to know each other, as long as it didn't take over completely. We encouraged them to keep building other kinds of connection, as well as explore their sexual connection, so they wouldn't get too distracted by limerence.

They'd had a few other small misunderstandings that we helped them clear up in coaching. In the process, they got better at identifying the assumptions they were each making, and learned to ask each other more direct questions, rather than assume.

For instance, one night when Cherie was going to Jill's house for dinner, she had offered to bring a salad. Jill had automatically responded, "Oh, you don't have to bring anything." Cherie felt a little hurt, and didn't bring the salad. Meanwhile, Jill had expected Cherie to bring the salad, even though she told her not to, so she didn't make one.

Although they had a perfectly fine dinner without salad, both women ended up feeling a little wary and confused about the interaction. When they talked about it, they got a lot of insight.

"I guess I was just being the kind of hostess my mother taught me to be," Jill said ruefully. "She always told guests not to bring anything, but then afterward, she always complained that they hadn't brought things!"

Cheri laughed. "Now at least I understand it wasn't personal. In the future, if you ever do that again, I'll just bring something anyway."

Once they talked about it, Jill realized that Cherie actually liked to make a contribution to their dinner. She also realized that she liked having Cherie contribute! In the past, she had actually trained her partners to let her be the provider, but at this point in her like she actually wanted a more mutual partnership, and so did Cherie.

In just a few sessions, Jill and Cherie became much more relaxed with one another around these kinds of small understandings, and much better able to unravel them on their own. Now, over a year later, their relationship is going strong.

CHAPTER 22

Changing Problematic Attraction Patterns: Sandy's Story

Sandy, 45, felt hopeless about creating the relationship she wanted. Her last relationship had ended 18 months before, and she was still hurting.

Sandy's ex June had pressured Sandy for months to give up her apartment and move into June's house. Yet when Sandy finally made the move, June broke up with her just six months later.

Sandy felt victimized by June, but she was smart enough to see the pattern. Her ex-husband had been manipulative and controlling, too, just like June.

Even worse, Sandy realized that she was attracted to women who had what she called an "edge." Women who were completely supportive and kind just didn't turn her on.

"I'm not a kid any more," Sandy said. "I want to make a life with someone. But what can I do if I'm always attracted to the wrong women?"

Despite feeling hopeless, Sandy was motivated enough to do her coaching homework. Week by week, we helped her make peace with her past, unravel her unhealthy attraction pattern, and prepare herself for lasting love.

As with Jeanette, a big part of Sandy's work involved self-love. We gave her a powerful practice to help her embrace her vulnerable younger self, and as she used it, she began feeling deep shifts.

We also helped Sandy tune in to what was really happening in her body – especially when she felt that attraction to "edgy" women. It turned out that when she got scared, she experienced it as lust. With tenderness, self-awareness and self-compassion, she became able to uncouple those feelings.

While doing coaching with us, Sandy met and dated three different women. She felt strongly attracted to the first woman, but by their third date, she recognized some major red flags. So, despite the attraction, Sandy stopped seeing her.

Bravo! We were thrilled for Sandy to have made this break in her pattern. (In the past, she admitted, she would have kept on going, red flags be damned – and of course, she would have paid the price in pain.)

When the second, Kerry, showed up, Sandy thought she might really be "the one." They had a picture-perfect first date in a fancy restaurant, and the woman pulled out her chair, paid the tab, and did all sorts of little things that made Sandy's heart flutter. Like Sandy, she was very successful in her career, so they seemed like a good match on that level.

However, on their second date, Sandy visited Kerry at her house, and clearly saw that Kerry wasn't yet over the breakup of her 20-year relationship. She didn't have a clear understanding of why the relationship had ended, and her house was still filled with mementos from her time with her ex.

Sandy felt compassion, but she also saw clearly that Kerry was not available. In fact, on further reflection, she realized that might have been part of why she'd felt so drawn to her. That felt a little discouraging.

So we helped Sandy work more deeply on formulating her relationship vision and then *opening herself up* – body, mind, heart and spirit – to that vision. Little by little, she became more able to believe that her life-long partner really was out there somewhere. "I haven't met her yet, but I can *feel* her," she told us.

We knew this was a very important step. We've seen over and over again that being able to fully envision *having what you want* seems to somehow open pathways in the universe.

Sandy now knew, and felt in her body, that *she had a right* to a healthy, loving relationship. She also knew it *was right* for her to have a healthy, loving relationship.

And she learned how to breathe through her fear when it came up, rather than having to turn it into lust. As she grew more gentle with herself, she also found herself able to imagine being attracted to a more gentle, and more fully available, woman.

A few weeks later, Sandy met Nicole at a party, and quickly realized that Nicole was an excellent match for her in many ways. In fact, she seemed like such a good match that Sandy worried she might not be attracted to Nicole, but as they continued dating, the chemistry blossomed.

During their first few months together, some of Sandy's fears and triggers resurfaced. For instance, on a camping trip the two women took together, Sandy got very triggered by something Nicole said. They ended up spending the afternoon apart, taking separate hikes so they could sort through their feelings. But when they met up again, they found themselves able to talk to each other honestly and openly, without blame.

Now Sandy and Nicole have moved in together, and their relationship feels stronger every day. Sandy often tells us, "I don't think this would have happened without Conscious Girlfriend."

CHAPTER 23

Ruth & Michelle's Story: The Craigslist Ad That Changed History (At Least, *Our* History)

Although it's very personal, we're including here the Craigslist ad Michelle posted back in March of 2006, and Ruth's initial response to that ad – because even though Conscious Girlfriend was eight years away from being formed, the ad and response do exemplify many of the principles we teach.

Yes, we were baby Conscious Girlfriends back then… and as you'll see, we were up-front about who we were from the very beginning. That's how we laid the groundwork for the deep and open love we've built.

We share this ad and response because:

- We hope you'll find it inspiring. After all, if the two of us could meet through Craigslist, of all places, it definitely shows that this universe is a magical place. *When you get ready, she shows up.*

- We hear "Is there anyone out there for me?" so often from the women we coach, and Michelle's ad was even headlined, "Are you out there?" So the answer on both counts is: *Yes.*

- Many women would shy away from posting an ad *or* writing an initial response this open and revealing. Yet it worked for us – and we believe it can work for you, too.

Michelle: *I posted this ad in the Women-Seeking-Women section on the San Francisco Bay Area Craigslist in March 2006. It had come to me, fully formed, while I was meditating a few days before. Being a good meditator, I gently pushed it away and went back to following my breath. A few days later, again while I was meditating, it came back – so I sighed, went to my computer, typed it up and posted it, and then went back to following my breath.*

Although Conscious Girlfriend was many years away, I can see now that actually, according to what I now know, I did a lot of things right even then. My ad presented a clear picture of who I was and what mattered to me, and described some key parts of my relationship vision.

Michelle's Craigslist Ad

Are You Out There? – 46, Berkeley

What follows is a description of a woman that I'd really like to meet. Of course, this is as much a description of me, as it is the woman I'm looking for.

You take life and the world very seriously, but you have a great sense of humor. You've probably been an activist at one point or another in your life, and you care deeply for the world and human beings, and want the world to be a better place. You also care deeply about God/Spirit/ultimate reality/awakening, and that is pretty much the center of your life, whether in a religious sense (as a member of an organized religion, as I am) or in a more informal way. One of these or both (world/spirit) is probably your life's work (as they have been for me.)

You are probably between 35 and 55. You are maybe butch, maybe femme, maybe somewhere in between, you maybe even discard those labels as useless, irrelevant, or patriarchal (I identify as butch, but only on some days, the other days I think labels are problematic.) Your most sensual organ is your brain, but it's not always like that - you need your heart and spirit to be involved, too. You appreciate and embrace the very wide range of the Bay Area's gay/lesbian/trans culture, but you likely are some-what on the crunchy-granola-vanilla side of things. You are likely to be a woman of color, but you might not be (I'm African-American.)

You love to read. On any trip to the beach (even for a day) you bring at least 2 books, one a novel or book of poetry, the other a non-fiction book about some topic you know well, or are just newly exploring. You like to write, and enjoy written correspondence, either the old fashioned way, or by email. You journal. You might even write a blog, perhaps. You have a real appreciation for the arts, and you might even be creative yourself. You love music, and you like to explore new artists and new kinds of music. You can even appreciate the value of a musical genre that you might not choose to listen to. You love movies, and you can appreciate the silly and the sublime, although you probably generally avoid horror films. You might like to cook - but you at least like really good food and generally go for healthy food. (I love to cook good food.)

You love to have conversations. Conversations about the state of the world, about theological/spiritual topics, about what kind of berries are best and why, and about relation-ships, and why any one that you are in at the present, is important to you and feeds you (or, doesn't).

You like to talk about how you feel. You like to be aware of another person's feelings. You love to listen, you are curious about others' perspectives, points of view, and feelings. You bring to any relationship a sense of generosity and respect. You have a network of friends that you nurture, and care deeply about. You probably don't have kids, or, if you do, they've grown up.

You've either actively thought about, or live, a life of relative simplicity, understanding that in order for human beings to survive on this planet, each of us, especially here, need to live in a smaller footprint. You might even have thought about, or live (or have lived) in intentional community of some sort. You've traveled to other countries, and other parts of North America, and find traveling an important part of your life. You might feel the need to get out of the US (even only to Canada or Mexico) at least once every couple of years, to see things from different perspectives.

You argue with yourself about the usefulness of Craigslist or other online dating sites to find someone like yourself. You have, at points, decided it's not really worth it, and have abandoned the effort. But then you find out a good friend of yours just had a date with someone she met on CL who seems really neat. So you decide to try again.

I don't need a picture, although if you request one, I'll gladly send one. Be prepared to have an engaging conversation by email first.

Ruth: *When I read Michelle's ad, I instantly knew: This is the next person I'll be with. There were so many quirky things she mentioned — including poetry and berries. It was just so clear to me that the ad had been written for me.*

284

And, of course, it turned out that I was right.
Here's what I responded.

Wow – what a great ad. I rarely check women-seeking-women on CL because the posts are usually so terrifyingly inane... so I even more rarely (far more rarely) answer. But what you wrote sounded quite astonishingly like me – I am truly amazed at how much alike we seem to be, at least in this two-dimensional forum, and in those aspects capable of being described by words. I hope we'll get to at least meet for tea to see if we click in some way – whatever way that might be.

I do take life very seriously – I am deeply reverent – and I am also deeply irreverent. Yes, I used to be an activist way back when, and these days I believe the real action is on the inner planes – transforming the self as a portal into transforming the world. I'm also a therapist/healer practicing in a non-traditional modality which incorporates aspects of Buddhism, shamanism, transpersonal psychology and energy medicine, so I don't just work on my own "inner plane" but help others work with theirs, as well.

Definitely, spirituality is at the absolute center of my life and core of my being. I've done a huge amount of emotional healing and spiritual work in the last few years, and it's been an amazing and very exciting ride. I was an old soul to begin with, but now I'm... well, a much clearer and healthier old soul. My major spiritual practice is a kind of hybrid of meditation and shamanic journeying, and my guides are also both reverent and irreverent. I figure a good way to know for sure that I'm tapping into a higher place is when it has a sense of humor.

I'm 44 – often told I look 5 or 10 years younger. People would mostly describe me as femme because I'm built small, and have long hair. But I'm sturdy and down-to-earth and extremely capable and competent, and insist on carrying everything myself. Butchy femme, maybe? I'm not much into labels but do tend to be attracted to women who look outwardly more butch than I do. I'm not a woman of color, though – I'm white, Jewish by ancestry though I don't especially identify that way. I'm fluent in Spanish and my longest-term relationship (7 ½ years) was with a Latina.

I do love to read – and how amazing that you even mentioned poetry. I have a vast collection of poetry. I identified as a poet for many years and published four books of it myself. As part of my spiritual process over the past few years I seem to have reached the other side of that shore, in terms of my own creative expression, but I'm definitely still a writer and am trying to shape the non-fiction book I'll write next… about healing and spirituality, though I have much to do to focus that theme. *(Author's Note: This book,* Soul on Earth: A Guide to Living & Loving Your Human Life, *was published in 2012.)*

And I do love good food – and healthy food. Both cooking it myself, and being cooked for (a pleasure I've too rarely had.) Hmmm, okay, where DON'T I fit your description? I can't truly say that I love movies. I'm too particular. But, I do love the movies that I love. When a movie really resonates for me, moves me, I'm happy to see it over and over again. I just find that that happens fairly rarely for me. But perhaps we would have similar taste. As you'd probably guess, I mostly like foreign and/or independent type films.

I loved Amores Perros. Y Tu Mama Tambien was pretty good. I loved Winged Migration and saw it about 5 times.

I love birds, animals, insects, and everything about nature more than just about anything else in the world. And berries – I can't believe you mentioned berries. I love picking blackberries in the Oakland/Berkeley hills – a major meditative act for me.

And yes, I've traveled quite a bit. Mostly have spent a lot of time in Latin America – also did some consulting work many years ago, when I was an AIDS educator, in Swaziland (Africa) and in the Caribbean.

Yes on listening, conversing, curiosity and respect. And on having a deep and wide network of friends and connections in the world. And on living simply, and intentionally.

I live in Oakland, in the ground floor in-law apartment of a big house I'm grateful to have bought many years ago with an ex-partner. There is something of an informal "intentional community" living upstairs – my teacher in the shamanic/energy medicine work, for whom I have great love and respect, teaches upstairs in my huge living room (though doesn't live here), and several other students of hers, also spirituality/healing minded types, live on the top floor. I've got a black and white cat and a huge wild back yard and a wonderful little meditation hut/therapy office hidden among the trees.

One thing I do want to mention right up front – because it is an issue for many women – is that although all of my relationships since age 20 have been with women, I did some major healing work over the past few years and reclaimed my attraction to men as a valid and non-threatening part of my being. I haven't been in an actual relationship for 2 ½ years now, but during that time I've had a few brief (six weeks was the longest) dating relationships with guys (as well as one with a woman). I have a hard time using the word "bisexual," both because I identified as lesbian for so many years, but also, more importantly, because the real internal movement for me is away from labels and identifications at all – and toward openness, fluidity toward all of life. So that's where I'm coming from with that.

Hope to hear back from you... and thanks again for the depth and thoughtfulness of your post.

-- Ruth

Two days passed before I heard back from Michelle. I thought, "Maybe I scared her off." But my gut knew better. It turned out that she was just sick. Then she answered me, we started emailing, met two weeks later, and lived happily ever after.

Well, not quite...

What Happily-Ever-After Really Looks Like

In our 9+ years of love, we've been through all sorts of challenges: cross-country moves, career changes, health crises, financial troubles, sexual healing and more. But through it all, we have remained deeply connected, loving, respectful and appreciative of each other. We genuinely adore each other, and we have a life together that's far sweeter, richer and more intimate than either of us could ever have imagined.

Really, it's amazing: a kid who grew up with her parents hurling insults and screaming at each other, and a kid who grew up feeling unloved, defective and broken, traveling a long winding road full of pain and breakups, and then finally finding our way to truly happy, healthy, lasting love.

That's why we know that if we can do it, you can, too.

It's also why Michelle proposed to me in March 2014, and I accepted. We got married on September 13, 2014, in a small, sweet ceremony with about twenty friends, down at the river beach in our back yard.

Because we are who we are, our ceremony didn't look like any wedding we've ever attended. In fact, it was a bit more like a workshop! We passed a talking stick I had made and invited each person to speak openly about their experiences, hopes and fears around love and marriage. Then we exchanged our vows, gave each other small handmade gifts, and took a break for a swim.

Ruth: *For many years, the idea of marriage scared me because I thought it would mean giving up part of who I was, or who I might want to become, to try to meet someone else's needs. So when Michelle proposed, I was surprised that I actually burst into tears.*

I was able to say Yes to her because the eight years we'd already spent together had shown me that committing myself to her wouldn't ever mean leaving myself behind. Whatever I want for myself, that's what she wants for me. And I honor her desires and needs in the same way.

Here are the vows we read to each other:

Ruth's Marriage Vows

I vow to behold you – and myself – with wonder, curiosity, tenderness, compassion and humor, and to embody my adoration, acceptance and respect for you.

I vow to tell the microscopic and inarguable truth to you and with you, and to bring my full consciousness and heart into our love and our life together.

I vow to cherish our shared path, even as I also honor your path as distinct from mine, and my path as distinct from yours.

I vow to honor and hold in my heart all of your many aspects: female and male, human and non-human, wounded and healed, past and present and still to be born – so that I can fully love you as you are in each moment, and also as you shift, change and evolve.

I vow to allow you to truly see me, know me and love me – to expose myself ever more fully to your gentle, wise, capacious mind, spirit and heart.

I vow to use my marriage to you as a way to deepen my connection to life on earth, and to use the support of our love to help me fulfill my purpose on this planet.

I vow to stand unwaveringly in support of your joy and of my own.

Michelle's Marriage Vows

I promise to continually discover the truths of who you are, to keep learning and honoring your life's purpose and path as I learn and honor mine.

I promise to share with you the two spirits in my body, and to grow to fully accept all of who I am so that I can fully receive your love, as I grow to love you more fully.

I promise to honor this land, the river and the trees, the grass and the flowers, the squirrels, deer, coyote and quail, the chickens, and horses, all that holds us both in the bounty and love of this Earth.

I promise to honor our autonomy and our closeness, to give you space when you ask, and take space when I need to, and to be willing to ask for closeness when I desire it.

I promise to honor the way that I am home for you, and appreciate the way you are home for me.

I promise to cultivate loving-kindness, generosity, healing, openness and curiosity in my life, and in our life together.

I deeply cherish you, who you are, our history, and the life we've led, and the marriage we are making. I look forward to our life together with joy, gratitude, and deep appreciation.

Our vows are unique to us, just as the particular forms and flavors of our love are a reflection of who we are. And when you find the partner who's right for you, and reach the point of making vows to one another – if you choose to do so – your vows will be unique to you. We hope you'll email them to us!

In Conclusion

Every single one of us is messy and imperfect – or, as I said earlier, a funny-looking mutt with some bad habits. But real love has room for all of our imperfections and limitations, as well as all of our strengths, gifts, beauty and magnificence.

A conscious partnership helps you grow in ways that allow you to feel enduring love, appreciation and compassion for another messy, imperfect human being – and also let in the enduring love, appreciation and compassion she feels for you. And it's the most profound, exciting adventure there is.

She is out there! And you are in here. *And both are equally important.*

By growing your ability to love yourself, befriend your feelings, and make peace with the past, you get yourself ready for happy, healthy love with someone else.

By growing your ability to speak and listen cleanly, dismantle your triggers, and stop fights in their tracks with the SCORE Process, you get yourself even *more* ready.

By learning the truths and busting the myths about chemistry and compatibility, you prepare yourself to date wisely.

By formulating a clear relationship vision, you become able to tell who's right for you, and who's not – and because of all the other skills you've already developed, you can turn away from the women who are wrong for you, and consciously choose to develop your connection with a woman who may be right.

Lasting, happy, healthy love is a journey. But you can get there! All it really takes is finding the right partner – and *being* the right partner, too. We're here to help you do both.

Wishing you much compassion, clarity, lesbian love and joy!

xoxo

Ruth & Michelle

Made in the USA
Coppell, TX
24 November 2019

11849084R00182